LANDMARK V

Nort

Cyprus

Kristina Gürsoy & Lavinia Neville Smith

Foreword

In writing this book we hope to have set out a guide that will inform and entertain. The most important objective for us was to produce the guide that both of us would like to have found when we first came to Cyprus. A guide that would take us from place to place and point out the best parts to be visited, especially for those who may only come to the island once.

However, Cyprus has a way of luring people back again, so there is plenty in this book for the second- or third-time visitor. Indeed Turkish folklore says that once you have visited Cyprus, you will return seven times!

We hope you have as much pleasure from reading this guide as we have had from writing it and that you thoroughly enjoy your time in Northern Cyprus. *Hoş geldiniz* – Welcome.

We would like to extend grateful thanks to all those who have wittingly or unwittingly contributed to this book and especially to Niyazi Gürsoy, Sarah Stephenson, Pat Lockhart, Christina Hessenberg and Lucienne Sumner-Fergusson.

Warning

Very few of the historical sites have adequate safety measures. There are unguarded drops and open cisterns to snare the unwary.

All visitors are advised to exercise extreme caution especially those with children.

KYRENIA/GIRNE CASTLE *(page 52)*

This originally French-built castle, enlarged and strengthened by the Venetians, houses the world famous Shipwreck Museum and is definitely 'a must' for visitors to Girne.

SALAMIS RUINS *(page 114)*

The visible remains of this once fabulously wealthy city, have been carefully restored and in places rebuilt by the archaeologists to give an insight into what life had to offer the citizens of the powerful Roman Empire.

BELLAPAIS ABBEY *(page 58)*

Of all the Gothic ruins in North Cyprus, Bellapais Abbey lives up to its' name of 'Abbey of Peace' and it is the most tranquil place in the north of the island.

ST MAMAS, GÜZELYURT *(page 146)*

A tax problem, or an ear, nose or throat infection send people flocking to the Church of St Mamas to seek help from this very popular saint. This church dedicated to him is the most beautiful and best preserved of the Orthodox churches that are now open as icon museums, it also contains the most exquisite crystal chandeliers.

KANTARA CASTLE *(see page 85)*

The most romantic of the mountain castles, and the castle of 101 rooms. The finder of the 101st room is guaranteed entry to Paradise. So says the legend.

Greece
Turkey
Crete
CYPRUS
Lebanon
Mediterranean Sea
Syria
Israel
Egypt

Landmark Publishing would like to thank the Turkish Republic of Northern Cyprus Ministry and Deputy Prime Ministry of State and especially Mr Orhan Tolun, Director of the Tourism Ministry for supplying the material upon which the maps in this book are based.

Opposite: Kampanopetra Basilica, Salamis

LANDMARK VISITORS GUIDE

Northern
Cyprus

Kristina Gürsoy & Lavinia Neville Smith

· CONTENTS ·

The island of Cyprus is the third largest in the Mediterranean Sea and the most easterly. It has a population of approximately 1,000,000, three-quarters of them in the southern half of the island. This is an island divided by differences of culture, politics and religion. The rift thus created has made the northern part of the island one of the most tranquil, uncluttered and uncommercialised holiday destinations in Europe.

Due to its position, close to the trade routes of the ancient civilised world, Cyprus has always been a bone of contention between the powers ruling the Mediterranean countries. Whether Phoenician, Greek, Roman, Byzantine, French or Ottoman, right through to the present day, each of the many different peoples have left an indelible imprint behind them.

There are artefacts made by man dating from 7,000BC. Cave dwellings dot the mountainsides and many of the villages still yield unexpected caches of pottery and ancient cooking utensils.

Whether the visitor is inclined towards history, wildlife, flowers, sunshine, sand or solitude, there is something on Cyprus for just about everyone. However, if the visitor requires bright lights, discos and commercialism, they are not to be found here.

Cyprus is an island steeped in legend. Here was the birthplace of Aphrodite, the goddess of love; giants have walked here and left their imprint, most notably in the massif of the Five Finger Mountain. It was here that an artisan king called Pygmalion ruled, he carved a statue of a woman so beautiful that he fell in love with her and Aphrodite, feeling sorry for him, breathed life into her marble body. That legend lives on today after one or two stages of development in the form of the musical *My Fair Lady*.

A GEOGRAPHICAL OUTLINE

The island of Cyprus is situated in the north-eastern corner of the Mediterranean Sea between latitudes 34° 33' and 35° 41' north and longitudes 32° 15' and 34° 35' east.

Its nearest neighbours are Turkey 40 miles (64km) to the north, Syria 60 miles (97km) east, Lebanon 108 miles (174km) south-east and Egypt 230 miles (370km) south. The total area of the island is approximately 3,572sq miles (9,252sq km), with a coastline of 486 miles (782km), consisting of enchanting coves, rocky coast and long golden sandy beaches. Northern Cyprus covers a total area of 1,357sq miles (3,515sq km) or nearly one third of the whole island. It is some 150 miles (242km) wide and 40 miles (64km) deep approximately at its extreme points.

The most prominent feature is the northern range of mountains, known as the Kyrenia Mountains, or Beşparmak Mountains. It is a narrow range, approximately 80 miles (130km) long, running parallel to the coastline. Occupying an area of approximately 100sq miles (260sq km), it is composed predominantly of limestone, dolomite, and marble. The highest point is Mount Selvili, near the village of Lapta, at 3,357ft (1,023m).

The largest spring in the island is in this range near Beşparmak mountain. The fertile north coast is chiefly covered with olive and carob trees.

The Mesaoria plain, which lies in the centre of the island, between the Kyrenia Mountains and the Troodos Mountains in the south, is used for the production of cereal crops such as wheat, barley and oats. It is known as the breadbasket of Cyprus.

Mainly the effects of side pressures have formed the island's present shape during different geological ages. 'Capes' have been formed where the land has strength against the erosion of the sea and 'Gulfs' have been formed where the land was weaker and so gave way to erosion. There are two capes, Zafer Cape at the end of the Karpas Peninsula and Koruçam Cape to the west. The two gulfs are at Güzelyurt and Gazimağusa.

GETTING THERE

Due to the fact that the Turkish Republic of Northern Cyprus (TRNC) is not recognised as a valid state, it is necessary to make a stopover in Turkey when flying to your holiday destination airport of **Ercan**.

The stopovers usually take place at one of the following airports: Izmir, Istanbul, or Antalya. The stopover, in general, is of about an hour's duration and, in the case of Cyprus Turkish Airlines and Istanbul Airlines, passengers are not normally required to change aircraft.

However, when travelling with Turkish Airlines there is nearly always a change of aircraft and sometimes a stopover at Istanbul Airport. Passengers are required to wait in the transit lounge and obtain a boarding pass for their on-going flight to Cyprus. It must be pointed out that if they make the mistake of going through 'passport control' they will be required to pay a £10 visa charge. This is because theoretically they will have entered the country. There is no such necessity for transit passengers.

Tour operators

There are many tour operators offering 'all in' holidays inclusive of flights and accommodation, or it is quite easy to book a flight only and rent accommodation privately. It must be said that the latter tends to be quite expensive in the long run, especially for families.

There are also tour operators offering specialist holidays tailored to suit archaeologists, botanists, walkers etc.

On arrival at Ercan airport the visitor will have his passport stamped with an entry visa for the TRNC. Contrary to popular belief among first time visitors to Northern Cyprus, having an entry visa in the passport does not prevent entry to either the Republic of Cyprus or any of the Greek Islands or mainland. The immigration officer in South Cyprus may, if he wishes, request permission from the visitor to 'cancel' the TRNC stamp. It is possible to request a separate form, which must be filled in by the passport holder with their personal details. This will then be stamped on entry and exit, it does however make the arrival procedure through immigration much longer and more tedious for all concerned.

Visitors who are travelling with a reputable tour company either to an hotel, holiday complex or villa are usually met by a company representative with transport that will take them to their destination. All tour operators provide transfers for visitors from the airport to the hotel of choice and also on their return. Distances from the airport are approximately Girne (Kyrenia) 23 miles (37km), Gazimağusa (Famagusta) 32 miles (51km) and Lefkoşa (Nicosia) 7 miles (11km).

Independent travellers

If the visitor has elected to find their own way, there are plenty of taxis to be found plying their trade at the airport. The fare is fixed and should be the equivalent of approximately US$42 or £25 to Girne or Gazimağusa and US$25 or £15 to Lefkoşa. There is no recommended bus from the airport.

HISTORY

For the visitor to understand and fully appreciate the island's many historical sites a short introduction to 9,000 years of habitation is very beneficial

Early settlers

The earliest settlers most probably came from the nearby Mediterranean countries clearly visible from Cyprus' shores. Small boats would have made the easily navigable journey – the Taurus Mountains of Turkey are only 40 miles (64km) from the island's north coast.

Artefacts found in the early settlements have clear links with similar finds on the mainland and there are many villages dating from the Neolithic to the Chalceolithic periods dotted throughout the island. The dwellings of the early inhabitants tended to be shelter partly provided by nature and added to where necessary. The village of **Vrysin** (within the Acapulco complex east of Girne) has dwellings partly sunk into the ground and walled with stone and mud brick. Ayios Epiktitos, now called **Çatalköy**, consisted of many cave dwellings, a large number of which are still easy to find.

A lack of settlements dating from the mid-Neolithic period (6000-4500BC approximately) make it impossible to say that the island was occupied during that time. It is, however, well proven with a wealth

NORTH CYPRUS

Mediterranean Sea

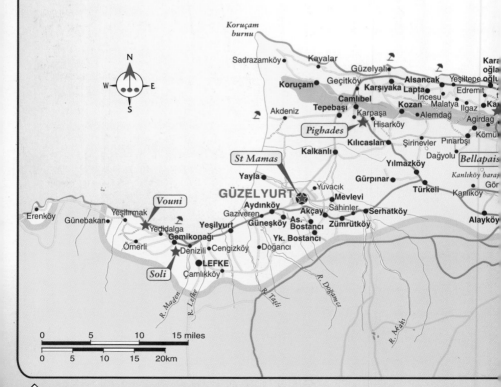

Koruçam burnu

N W E S

Sadrazamköy
Kayalar
Güzelyalı
Kara oğla
Koruçam
Geçitköy
Karşıyaka
Alsancak
Yeşiltepe oğlu
Lapta
Edremit
İncesu
Çamlıbel
Kozan
Malatya
Ilgaz
Ka
Akdeniz
Tepebaşı
Karpaşa
Alemdağ
Agirdag
Hisarköy
Kömü
Pighades
Kılıcaslan
Şirinevler
Pınarbşı
Kalkanlı
Dağyolu
Bellapais
Yılmazköy
Kanlıköy baraj
St Mamas
Gürpınar
Gör
Yayla
Türkeli
Kanlıköy
GÜZELYURT
Yuvacık
Mevlevi
Vouni
Aydınköy
Akçay
Şahinler
Serhatköy
Erenköy
Yeşilırmak
Gaziveren
As. Bostancı
Zümrütköy
Alayköy
Günebakan
Yedidalga
Yeşilyurt
Güneşköy
Gemikonağı
Cengizköy
Doğancı
Ömerli
Denizili
Yk. Bostancı
Soli
LEFKE
Çamlıkköy

R. Maden
R. Lefke
R. Tasli
R. Doğancı
R. Maki

| 0 | 5 | 10 | 15 miles |
| 0 | 5 | 10 | 15 | 20km |

Buffavento Castle overlooking the Mesaoria plain

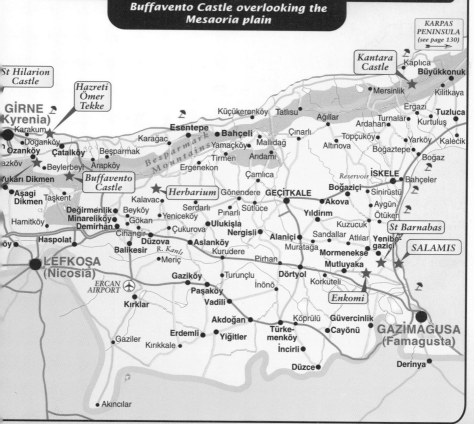

KARPAS
PENINSULA
(see page 130)

St Hilarion Castle

Hazreti Ömer Tekke

GİRNE (Kyrenia)

Karakum

Doğanköy

Ozanköy Çatalköy Beşparmak

azköy Beylerbeyi Arapköy

Yukarı Dikmen Buffavento Castle

Aşagi Dikmen Taşkent Kalavac

Hamitköy Değirmenlik Beyköy
Minareliköy Gökan
Demirhan Cihangir

Haspolat Düzova Çukurova

öy Balikesir R. Kanlı
Meriç

LEFKOŞA (Nicosia) Gaziköy Turunçlu

ERCAN AIRPORT Paşaköy

Kırklar Vadili

Akdoğan

Gaziler Erdemli Yiğitler
Kırıkkale

Akıncılar

Esentepe

Karağac Bahçeli
Yamaçköy Mallıdağ
Tirmen Arıdamı
Ergenekon Çamlıca

Herbarium Gönendere GEÇİTKALE
Serdarlı Pınarlı Sütlüce
Yeniceköy
Ulukışla
Nergisli Alaniçi
Aslanköy Sandallar
Kurudere Murataga
Pirhan
İnönö Dörtyol Korkuteli

Köprülü Güvercinlik
Türke- Cayönü
menköy
İncirli

Düzce

Küçükerenköy Tatlısu

Ağıllar Turnalar
Ardahan
Topçuköy Altınova Boğaztepe

Reservoir İSKELE

Boğaziçi Sinirüstü
Akova Aygün
Ötüken
Yıldırım
Kuzucuk Atılar Yenibo-
gaziçi
Mormenekse
Mutluyaka

Enkomi

Kantara Castle Kaplıca
Büyükkonuk
Mersinlik Kilitkaya
Ergazi Tuzluca
Kurtuluş
Yarköy Kalecik
Boğaz

Bahçeler

St Barnabas

SALAMIS

GAZİMAGUSA (Famagusta)

Derinya

Beşparmak Mountains

Çınarlı

STONE AGE	
Neolithic I	7,000 – 6,000BC
Neolithic II	4,500 – 3,900BC
Chalceolithic	3,900 – 2,600BC
BRONZE AGES	
Early	2,300 – 1,850BC
Middle	1,900 – 1,600BC
Late	1,600 – 1,050BC
IRON AGES	
Geometric	1,050 – 750BC
Archaic	750 – 475BC
Classical	475 – 325BC
Hellenistic	325 – 58BC
Roman	58BC – 330AD
Byzantine	330 – 1191
French	1191 – 1489
Venetian	1489 – 1571
Ottoman	1571 – 1878
British	1878 – 1960
Independent Cyprus	1960 – 1974
Turkish forces intervention	1974
TRNC	1983

of artefacts and villages that the people from the Chalceolithic period flourished (3900-2600BC). They discovered copper and found it a product that was exportable, thus beginning the trade routes from Cyprus that were to become so important in future centuries.

The people of this time were hunters, fishermen and artisans. The pottery of the period stands well in comparison with its modern counterpart and some looks as fresh as if it had just come from the potter's kiln.

Expansion and trade

The Early and Middle Bronze Ages (2300-1600BC) saw the first real towns and commercial centres de-veloping. The export of copper expanded into Egypt and Asia Minor and cultural relations and contacts with neighbouring countries continued to improve.

Much of the shipping went through the port of **Enkomi** and it has long been thought that Enkomi identifies with the town of Alasia referred to in ancient texts. However, inscriptions on fourteenth century BC tablets found at Tell el Armana in Middle Egypt cast doubt upon this theory. Currently being examined, they seem to pin-point the copper-rich capital of Alasia as being one of two towns, Alassa Paleotaverna or Kalavassos Ayiosdemetrios in the southern side of the Troodos Mountains. Final proof has yet to be established. What is known is that the word copper is derived from the Greek *kipris* meaning 'Cyprus' so the two have long been synonymous.

The Mycenaean peoples who continued the development of cities around the island, such as Enkomi in the north and **Paphos** in the south, brought Greek cultural methods with them and this shows in the style of the highly decorative pottery that has been found. They started to produce figurines, vases, highly decorative plates etc. These were produced not just for the home and domestic market but also for export. Much as we would find in a china shop of today, so the late Bronze Age traders were selling statues, not of pop idols and princes but of gods and goddesses of their pagan culture, horses, chariots and various animals. Designs feature strongly on their plates, bowls and other household vessels.

The continued prosperity and cultural growth of the people during the late Bronze Age appears to have been disrupted by a turbulent time when the island came under attack from a distant culture that has never been identified. These people are referred to as 'The Sea People' and where they came from and returned to is a matter of pure conjecture. During this time many cities were destroyed and rebuilt, fortified or abandoned. After causing considerable trouble and turbulence 'The Sea People' disappeared as mysteriously as they had arrived.

At around this time Achaen settlers landed on the northern coast at what is now called the Achaens' Beach and began the colonisation which links the cities of Salamis, Soli, Paphos and others with heroes from the siege of Troy. They brought with them their cultures and their pagan gods. Terracotta figures of both male and female deities bear strong resemblance to those found around Mycenae and Crete.

The Iron Age

The next stage in development was the Iron Age. Leading up to this, various natural disasters, such as earthquakes, slowed down growth and led to a dispersal of the people and a downturn in trade. The inhabitants who continued to live on Cyprus carried on their traditions, and with the arrival of the Phoenicians, trade and industry received a much-needed boost. The island began to gather economic strength especially as links with the Orient became established. Religion started to change and the Horned God much favoured by the Mycenaeans was replaced by the cult of the Goddess Astarte, the Goddess of Fertility. She in due course was replaced

by the Goddess Aphrodite, who too is connected with love and fertility and is also considered a native of Cyprus.

During the following three hundred years the island came under the domination of Near Eastern rulers and for a brief period of about twenty years the island paid dues to the Kingdom of Assyria then for forty years to the Egyptians. After this the Persian Empire took control of Cyprus and permitted several of the city-states that arose at this time the right to mint their own coinage. These included Lapithos (Lapta), Soli and Salamis.

The pottery of this time, with its depiction of floral motifs and mythical creatures, strongly reflects the eastern influence of the Phoenicians.

Worship expanded to include gods of the Egyptians, Greeks and Phoenicians. Terracotta figures that obviously represent deities have been found on the island, most notably at **Akdeniz** where some 2,000 figures set round an altar were discovered in a *temenos* (see Glossary, page 189).

Persian rule

The dawn of the Classical period saw an attempt by the islanders to throw off the rule of Persia, with the result that large areas in rebellion were defeated and only parts of the island were freed. The Greeks continued to regard Cyprus as a rich source of timber and other materials and struggled vigorously to maintain only a tenuous hold on the island until the arrival of Evagoras. As a descendent of Teucer, the founder of **Salamis**, Evagoras

(cont'd on page 16)

The beautiful thirteenth century French Gothic abbey of Bellapais – the Abbey of Peace

• Cyprus —

Legend and reality blend together on the island of Cyprus where Aphrodite, the Goddess of Love, emerged from the foaming waves of the shores of Paphos and impressed upon Cyprus the seal of eternal beauty. Maybe this is why Cyprus has also been called the 'Sweet Land'.

Throughout the ages people of various lands have used many different names for Cyprus. The origin of the name is obscure. It has been referred to as '*makaria*' which means blissful and '*aspelia*' which means well adorned. In medieval times it was called 'The Island of Saints', because of the island's many saints and the piety of the people. Could the name have been derived from the yellow Cyprus sun rose flower growing on the island or from the copper, which was once found in abundance, or from the cypress tree?

Home of the gods

The Olympian gods: Zeus, Apollo, Poseidon, Dionysos, Hera, Athena, Aphrodite, Artemis and Demeter, other lesser gods and heroes, such as Asclepios, Persephone, Heracles, Leto and the Nymphs established themselves in Cyprus. The gods felt comfortably at home here, having found another mountain of Olympian heights, and settled on the highest peak of the Troodos Mountains.

Geologists say that the rocks of Cyprus were created during the Cretaceous period, which means they are 150 million years old. However legend tells us that when God created the world, He

claimed what he rightfully considered his, the throne of Salamis. He deposed the pro-Persian ruler Abdemon and yet succeeded in promoting good trading relations with the Persian Empire, continuing the development of Salamis as a commercial centre and powerful city. He also minted coinage at Salamis.

Unfortunately for him he stretched too far and when he attempted to take the whole island under his rule, the Persians took strong measures to prevent him. He was permitted to continue his rule of Salamis on condition that he paid dues to Persia. He was murdered circa 374BC and it was not until 325BC that Alexander the Great finally destroyed the Persian Empire and released Cyprus from the yoke of tyranny and constant fighting.

Hellenistic period

Alexander's great victories throughout Asia Minor culminated in the tossed from His hands lumps of clay which fell into the sea, from one of these Cyprus was created.

The centuries of vicissitudes have their explanation too: "God torments those He loves" or *"Allah peksemet'i dışsiz'e verir"*, which means "God gives the hardest crust to those without teeth."

Five Finger Mountain

There are many legends about the local landmarks and many concern the formation of the Five Finger (Beşparmak) mountain. One tells the story of a conceited villager who fell in love with the local 'queen' and asked for her hand in marriage. The queen wished to be rid of the impertinent young man and requested that he bring her some water from the spring of St Andreas monastery in the Karpas.

This was a perilous journey in those days. The man set off and after several weeks returned with a skinful of the precious water. The queen was most dismayed to see that he had succeeded, but still refused to marry him. In a fit of rage he poured the water onto the earth, seized a handful of the resulting mud and threw it at the queen's head. She ducked and the lump of mud sailed far across the plain to land on top of the Kyrenia Range, where it is to this day, still showing the impression of the thwarted villager's five fingers.

Dighenis

Another legend tells of the giant Byzantine hero, Dighenis, fleeing from his Arab pursuers. As he leapt across the sea he grasped the top of the mountain and left his hand print. Thus the Beşparmak mountain or Five Fingers.

siege of Tyre. Here, he was assisted by a huge flotilla of ships from Cyprus which helped to blockade the city. As a result, Cyprus was now able to enjoy a new found independence. This, however, was short lived as Alexander's death at the early age of thirty-three led to bitter fighting and rivalry between three of his Generals, each of whom felt that he was the only worthy successor to follow Alexander's great visionary leadership and rule his empire.

Eventually they agreed to divide the empire and two of the generals, Antigonus and Ptolemy, both claimed Cyprus. In 318 the latter made firm his control over the island but it was seized from him in 306 by Demetrius the son of Antigonus and it was not until eleven years later that Ptolemy was able to regain control.

During the rule of the first three Ptolemys, Alexandria became a great cultural and trade centre and this in due course had an effect on

Cyprus. Most notably, the local alphabet was replaced by the Greek.

Greek architecture flourished, though little remains today as Roman forums, theatres, market places etc. were built on the ruins and foundations of their Greek predecessors.

The end of the Hellenistic rule came when the rudeness of the last Ptolemy towards an eminent Roman Senator gave the Roman Empire an excuse to annex the island and it became a Roman province.

Roman period

The first Governor from Rome was Marcus Portius Cato who had the task of implementing the annexation of the island. He arrived in 58BC and began almost four hundred years of Roman rule.

Due to far-sighted tax reforms first initiated by Julius Caesar and continued by Augustus, the treasury of the Roman Empire was very well off. This allowed vast sums to be spent for the benefit of the public, pleasing the people who no longer felt so oppressed by the greed of the tax collectors. Before the reforms tax collectors had been lining their own coffers with the money collected and not passing it all to the treasury in Rome.

Prosperity

The benefits to Cyprus were innumerable. New harbours were built for continued trading all round the island. Water was channelled to all the major cities by massive aqueducts. The one to Salamis from the spring in the Kyrenia Mountain was 35 miles (56km) long. New roads were laid with Roman precision. Theatres and market places were built for the entertainment of the populace and for them to trade their goods. Cities with well-frequented harbours flourished; in particular Salamis became incredibly rich through its exports to other markets of the Roman Empire.

It was at Salamis that St Paul and St Barnabas converted the Roman Governor Sergius Paulus to Christianity, making him the first Christian ruler in the world. The mission of Barnabas and Paul was to spread the message of Christianity throughout the Roman Empire, and the fact that Barnabas was a native Cypriot had great influence on the Church of Cyprus achieving its independence from the See of Antioch.

Barnabas' fate was unpleasant to say the least. He was murdered by being stoned to death by the native Jews of Salamis whilst he was preaching in the city. The Jews continued their uprising against the spread of Christianity eventually inciting full scale rebellion around 110AD when it is reported that they succeeded in slaughtering over 250,000 local Christians. This rebellion was put down by the Emperor Trajan, and all Jews were expelled from the island.

The next half century saw a prosperous island. However during the gradual collapse of the Roman Empire the island had a downturn in its fortunes recovering only under Constantine the Great, who made tremendous efforts to hold his empire together under firm Christian rule. Towards the end of the fourth century earthquakes destroyed many of the major cities including Salamis. Renamed Constantia after the Emperor Constantius II, the city was partly rebuilt, though never again achieved its former splendour.

Byzantine rule

The split within the Roman Empire brought Cyprus under the rule of Byzantium with the capital city being Constantinople, and the eastern empire ruled from Alexandria. Constantine approved Christianity as the official religion throughout the empire and this spread rapidly.

Barnabas, patron saint of Cyprus

Cyprus at this time came under the See of Antioch and the financial benefits to the Patriarch of that See were tremendous. The Bishops of Cyprus, anxious no doubt to keep the wealth on the island, requested a break from the jurisdiction of Antioch and asked to be granted independent status, with their own Archbishop.

The bishop of Constantia, Anthemios, was rewarded one night with a dream, in which he found the body of Barnabas, saint and one time native of Salamis. After his murder, the body of Barnabas had lain hidden for nearly four hundred years. Anthemios searched for the body and found it as had been shown in the dream. For the bishop, it was the miracle required to persuade the Emperor Zeno to allow the creation of the first patriarch. The Orthodox church of Cyprus was officially recognised in 488AD and a church was built and dedicated to Barnabas, who from then on has been the patron saint of Cyprus.

The commercial standing of Cyprus throughout the Byzantine Empire continued to increase. The Emperor Justinian considered it of enough importance to have the island classified as a province during the mid-sixth century. The next hundred years were quiet and prosperous with the increased production of silk which was sold throughout the Middle East.

Islamic raids

While the rest of the Mediterranean countries were battling against the Goths and Vandals, Cyprus' shores lay peaceful and undisturbed, until out of distant Arabia came marauding Islamic forces. They plundered many of the ancient cities and sacked, looted and burned anything that stood in their path. Many beautiful Christian buildings were destroyed and whole townships subsequently abandoned.

The raids continued for over two hundred years and the people were made to pay taxes to both Constantinople and whichever Caliph was in power at the time. This oppressive period did not end until the Byzantine Emperor defeated the Arabs and made the island secure again. It was during this period that some of the island's major fortifications were built, including the mountain castles of **Kantara**, **Buffavento** and **St Hilarion**.

For a short while there was renewed prosperity until the Turks swept to power by seizing Jerusalem and defeating the Byzantine Emperor.

Crusaders

During this era of chaos a nephew of Emperor Manuel Comnenus seized the island of Cyprus and had himself proclaimed Emperor, renouncing all allegiance to Constantinople. Isaac Comnenus was a despotic ruler, he treated the islanders brutally and was intensely disliked. His rule lasted only seven years and was brought to an end when he was foolish enough to capture Berengaria of Navarre, the future wife of Richard the Lionheart, King of England.

The Christian forces of Europe were on their way to try and stop the continuing spread of Islam after the defeat of Guy de Lusignan at Jerusalem in 1187. Some of these forces went by land and some by sea as they embarked on the Crusade against the bloody infidel, Saladin.

Richard travelled by sea and his fleet was scattered during a storm. Several came to ground on Cyprus' shores. One carrying Berengaria took refuge at Limassol and was captured by Isaac. He also imprisoned and ill-used all the sailors he managed to capture. Too late, he realised his mistake in provoking King Richard's wrath. Richard seized the town of Limassol and in turn captured Comnenus. The latter managed to escape and took refuge first at Kantara and then at the tip of the Karpas Peninsula where he was eventually recaptured by Guy de Lusignan who had come to join Richard's crusade.

After his wedding to Berengaria at Limassol in May 1191, Richard was able to take stock of the island he had captured and discovered that during his brief period of tyrannical rule, Comnenus had amassed considerable riches in his treasury. With this new-found wealth Richard was able to set off for Acre and renew his crusade. He departed the island, leaving a small garrison in charge.

Rebellious Cypriots

The soldiers had continual problems trying to control the islanders who had had enough of oppression and Richard realised that having taken all he could from the treasury the island was now more trouble than it was worth so he sold it to the Templar Knights.

After paying Richard a deposit they in turn found the rebellious Cypriot peasants too much to handle and asked Richard to cancel the purchase of the island. This he did, retaining the original deposit, and then sold it to Guy de Lusignan as some sort of compensation for the loss of Jerusalem.

Three hundred years of French rule

With Guy's purchase began a period of French rule that was to last for almost three hundred years.

French rule was as harsh as anything the Cypriots had endured before, with the introduction of a feudal system that granted power to the barons who had supported Guy during his battles in the Holy Land. There was a revised legal constitution which did, however, retain some local laws and customs.

Guy de Lusignan was never crowned King of Cyprus, the first monarch was Amalric, Guy's brother who came to power in 1194 and was granted the Crown of Cyprus by the Holy Roman Emperor, Henry IV in 1197.

In 1194 Guy died and was succeeded by his brother Amalric who became Lord of Cyprus and in 1197 was crowned and recognised as the first King of Cyprus. The French monarchs continued to hold the title King of Jerusalem and were crowned (*in absentia*) at the cathedral of St Nicholas in Gazimağusa. That church being the one closest to the Holy Land.

Other changes carried out by the French rulers included the oppression of the Orthodox religion, and the reduction of Orthodox Bishops. Although not totally forbidden, the Orthodox faith was pushed out into less wealthy areas and the great revenues amassed by the Orthodox Church were reallocated to the Church of Rome.

This act of religious suppression caused great anger among the native people and they distrusted their French overlords. There was a great contrast between the lifestyles of the locals and the newcomers, the latter living the highlife with flamboyant displays of wealth. The building of great churches and abbeys, the extensions of castles and palaces all demonstrated the divide between the native poor and their rich rulers. Over the next three centuries this was to change and the Cypriot people were to derive great benefit from French rule.

Amalric was succeeded by his son Hugh I in 1205. His rule ended after the Crusade of 1218 when he died the following year leaving a son, Henry, of only nine months to become king under the regency of the infant king's uncle, Philip of Ibelin, and his mother, Alice of Champagne.

It was not long before war broke out between Philip and Frederick II, the Holy Roman Emperor, who cast covetous eyes on Cyprus and wished to replace the regency with his own choice of bailiffs who would

control parts of the island and be loyal to him. However, in this Frederick was unsuccessful and two attempts to take control of the island failed and a victory at Agridi in June 1232 just as the young King Henry came of age assured the independence of the island. Henry I died in 1253 and his only son Hugh II died at the age of fourteen, leaving the crown to pass to a cousin who became Hugh III.

His reign is marked by the widespread interest in Western intellectual and cultural reforms. He was renowned for the brilliance of his court and for the fact that he spent most of his time in Cyprus and not journeying about the Mediterranean.

He was succeeded by his eldest son John I, who ruled for a brief two years. He in turn was succeeded by his brother Henry II. His was a reign marred by misfortunes. He suffered from epilepsy, a condition viewed with much suspicion at the time. He also lost his last mainland possession when Acre fell in 1291. He was continually falling out with his brother, Amalric Prince of Tyre. Eventually Amalric deposed him and had him deported to Armenia in 1310. In the same year Amalric was assassinated and the rightful king was restored to his throne.

The reigns of Hugh IV and Peter

In 1327 Henry II died and was succeeded by his nephew Hugh IV who became one of the great Kings of Cyprus. Despite being tyrannical and intolerant he was an inspired promoter of the arts and loved beautiful things. He was directly responsible for the building of the **Abbey at Bellapais**.

He was succeeded in 1359 by his son Peter I, and so began a short, but glorious reign. He had two great intellectuals to guide him during the early years of his rule. His chancellor Philip of Mézieres, who was a truly loyal servant, and also the papal legate, Peter Thomas.

Peter I had inherited his father's violent temper and a strong streak of immorality. However his excesses were kept well under control by his trusted advisers and they encouraged him to try to regain the kingdom of Jerusalem. He made the rounds of the courts of Europe raising money for his cause. He set off on his crusade in 1364 and captured Alexandria. Unfortunately his troops were interested only in the plunder they had captured and hastened to carry off the spoils; the commanding officers had no recourse but to withdraw leaving Peter I feeling bitter and angry.

He asked the courts to punish those who had retreated but the Barons of the High Court refused his plea.

In 1366 his most trusted councillor Peter Thomas died; his queen Eleanor was constantly unfaithful; the barons had all turned against him and Peter I gave himself up to his passions and excesses.

An end to this period of ignominious rule, which clouded an otherwise perfect reign was brought about when Peter I was assassinated by a baronial conspiracy in 1369.

Regency

There followed a period of regency more troubled than any other because the late king's only son was weak, sickly and not of age.

The regency fell to the evil, scheming Queen Eleanor, the boy king's mother and his two uncles, John, Prince of Antioch, and James the Constable.

The royal factions set up deep divisions within the council and these rifts widened with old, ongoing feuds between the Genoese and Venetians who had long been granted privileges at the royal court.

The task of holding the country together proved fruitless against people determined on waging a profitable war. During the festivities following the coronation of Peter II a brawl had broken out between the nobles of Genoa and Venice, which developed into a full scale battle. The Genoese landed in force in 1373 and put the island to the sack. The major towns and cities; the abbeys and churches were all plundered and the treasury robbed of its wealth. They maintained a hold on the city of Famagusta (Gazimağusa) but otherwise, having taken all they wanted and capturing James the Constable, they departed. The luckless young king continued to be ruled by his mother whose hatred for her brothers-in-law grew unchecked. She succeeded in having Prince John assassinated but could not get at James who was languishing in a jail in Genoa.

In 1382 the hapless Peter II died leaving no children from his marriage to Valentina Visconti daughter of the Duke of Milan.

Queen Eleanor had at last been sent into exile so could no longer interfere with the running of the country. The heir to the throne was James the Constable who was still in jail. He managed to raise the ransom demanded and returned to Cyprus to reorganise his kingdom.

This he did with a modicum of success and died in 1398. His son

Janus followed him and married Charlotte of Bourbon.

The country had started to become prosperous once more when, in 1426, the Egyptians invaded, probably incited by the Genoese. They almost annihilated Janus's army and took him prisoner. Cyprus then came under the vassalage of Egypt.

The end of the French kings

Janus died in 1432 to be succeeded by his totally weak and incompetent son who became John II. He was in turn dominated by his mistress, his wives and his bastard son James. His inglorious reign came to an end in 1458 and he was succeeded by his only legitimate child, Charlotte. She in turn was deposed by her bastard brother in alliance with the Sultan of Egypt.

The splendours of French rule were drawing rapidly to a close but James the bastard did make a last ditch attempt to preserve some of the glories of the past. He reorganised the kingdom he had usurped and drove the Genoese out of Famagusta. For money and allies he turned to Venice and married Catherine Cornaro.

James II died in what today would be described as suspicious circumstances and for which no adequate explanation was ever given. His posthumous son James III died at a year old and Catherine ruled as queen. For thirteen years she desperately held out against the might of Venice, eventually giving in to a power too strong to oppose. She abdicated in 1489 leaving Cyprus to become a Venetian stronghold.

Soli – one of the many animal motifs set in the mosaic floor of the basilica

The people of Cyprus did not wish to see an end to the dynasty that had ruled for the last three centuries. They had become used to the prosperity around them and did not relish the thought of rule from Venice. However any ideas of rebellion were swiftly crushed with harsh punishment.

Venetian rule

The Venetians wanted Cyprus for purely mercenary reasons. Its strategic position made it an ideal point from which Venice could dominate all eastern trade routes, and the island was a rich source of good timber for shipbuilding. To protect their asset, an immediate plan of heavy re-fortification took place. The mountain castles were dismantled to prevent them being used by any internal insurgent force and the major cities were redeveloped by the finest military architects in anticipation of attack from the Ottomans.

After coming to power in Cyprus the Venetians had continued to pay dues to the Mameluke Egyptians; however after the Egyptians had been conquered by the Ottomans, taxes were paid to Constantinople. It became increasingly obvious that the Ottomans would endeavour to conquer Cyprus and all possible measures were taken to prevent this happening.

The walls around the cities of Nicosia (Lefkoşa) and Famagusta (Gazimağusa) are strong testament to the talent of their military engineers and architects. The Venetians erected huge earthworks with dressed stone facings, interspersed at intervals with bastions from which to direct their cannon power.

Ottoman invasion

All their efforts eventually proved in vain, when after almost eighty years, in which building work had been the main project, the Ottomans landed at Larnaca in 1570. These forces, led by Lala Mustapha Paşa, put Nicosia (Lefkoşa) under siege. Terms of honourable surrender were placed before the Venetian commanders but these they resolutely refused to accept. The result was that Nicosia was taken after six weeks, with a huge majority of the inhabitants being massacred and the city looted. From the capital, the Ottoman forces marched towards Kyrenia (Girne). This city gave in without a shot, leaving only Famagusta (Gazimağusa) to be conquered.

The siege of Famagusta

The siege of Famagusta took ten long months, the walls of the city withstanding the assault of the Ottoman forces. The bravery and tenacity of the Venetians led by Marc Antonio Bragadino have been thoroughly chronicled by past historians. However, courage was not enough when the city ran out of supplies, and stores expected to arrive from Venice failed to materialise.

Eventually, despite causing heavy loss of life to the Ottoman forces, Bragadino was forced to capitulate and signed the terms of surrender in August 1571. After the surrender, trumped up charges were made against Bragadino with the result that he was arrested, imprisoned, tortured and then flayed alive. His treatment being seen by the public, making them realise the power of the Ottoman Empire was not to be thwarted.

Ottoman rule

The Ottoman period of rule began with some changes that most of the local population welcomed. The Catholic Church, long hated by Orthodox believers was thrown out and many of the churches were converted into mosques. In particular St Sophia in Nicosia, and St Nicholas in Gazimağusa. Now the Selimeye Mosque and Lala Mustapha Paşa Mosque respectively.

The Catholic church of Bellapais Abbey was handed over to the Orthodox faith, the remainder of the monastic buildings were unused and gradually fell into a state of dereliction.

The French feudal system was radically changed, allowing former vassals to be released from their vows of fealty and to own and inherit land.

The population of the island increased with settlement of Turks from the mainland, many of whom had been made gifts of land by the Sultan.

These favourable points were unbalanced by the system of government, which was conducted from Nicosia with two lesser offices in Paphos and Famagusta. The collection of taxes was administered by Agas who had purchased their positions from the Sublime Porte, which was the court of the Ottoman Empire. Naturally they were assiduous in their efforts to raise as much revenue as possible to cover their own expenses and still show a handsome profit which in turn was paid to Constantinople.

The Cypriots found themselves still under the yoke of oppression, and, as was to be expected, poverty and famine soon engulfed them. In the mid-seventeenth century a great plague further reduced the population to approximately 25,000.

Taxes were reduced and the Porte agreed to recognise the Orthodox Archbishops as the representative of the non-Muslim Cypriot people. This however did not improve the overall lot of the Cypriots very much, and it was not until 1754 that the Sultan agreed officially to accept the Orthodox Archbishop as the leader of the Cypriot community, granting him and his bishops certain privileges and generally in a small way improving the lot of the people.

Unrest, and massacre

The raising of taxes was now in the hands of the clergy. For a short time the system worked until once again the mercenary desire for money made the church greedy and both Greek and Turkish peasants revolted, albeit in vain. At the beginning of the nineteenth century it was discovered that an organisation was at work in secret with the connivance of the Orthodox Archbishop of Cyprus to drive all Turks out of Greece.

The action taken by the Turkish General of Cyprus was bloody and merciless. The Archbishop was massacred along with several bishops and there was a purge of Christians across the island. The Ottoman Empire was now experiencing trouble from within as one of its governors established an independent dynasty in Egypt and war with Russia continued. For almost a hundred years Russia had been chipping away at the borders of the Ottoman Empire and after first gaining access through the Bosporus they were then given parts of Anatolia.

British control

The British, worried that the Russians would pose a threat to the Suez canal, were quite happy to accept the offer of governorship proposed by the Ottomans. In 1878 agreement was reached and Cyprus came under British control and occupancy. Cyprus continued to be part of the Ottoman Empire and revenues were still paid annually to the Sultan after necessary expenditure had been deducted.

A new constitution was created, and a new high court was established. Two judges, one Christian and one Muslim presided.

The legislative council was modified in 1882, consisting of six British, nine Greek and three Turkish members, and considerable outrage was caused by the unfair proportions. The Turks, however, usually took the part of the British and the High Commissioner had the casting vote.

There was an extensive building programme consisting of new roads and bridges. New water pipelines for both drinking and crop irrigation, and a railway line was built to link Famagusta to Morphou (Güzelyurt) via Nicosia. From Morphou there was a branch line to service the copper mining area of Lefke.

In 1914 Turkey joined forces with Germany and the island was annexed to the British Crown. The agreement of 1878 was annulled and in 1915 Britain offered the island to Greece if they would fight on the side of the Allies in the World War I. The offer was refused. In 1925 the island became a Crown

Above: Local fisherman showing off his catch of the day

Opposite: Fresco of the Virgin Mary in the church of Panagia Theotokos at Yeni Iskele

colony under the control of a newly appointed governor.

Union with Greece

Enosis, union with Greece, which would have taken place had Greece accepted the British offer in 1915, now became an issue of paramount importance to the local people. An issue that was encouraged by the Orthodox Church, resulting in ferocious riots in 1931 when Government House was burnt to the ground.

After the rebellion had been crushed, the local voice of the people was silenced by the abolition of the Legislative Council. World War II saw an estimated 30,000 Cypriots fighting in the British forces with great loyalty and fervour. At the end of the war the call for *Enosis* was renewed. A plebiscite engineered by Archbishop Makarios in 1950 showed 96 per cent of Greek Cypriots in favour of Enosis. However it is doubtful, even if the voting percentage was accurate, that the majority of Cypriots knew what they were voting for.

EOKA and armed struggle

They did not want any more colonial rule, and the offer of a new constitution triggered the start of the armed offensive by EOKA (National Organisation of Cypriot Fighters) led by George Grivas against continuing British rule. This battle for self-rule started in April 1955 with the blessing of the Archbishop Makarios.

The request for Enosis was outlawed and Makarios was exiled to the Seychelles in June 1956. His exile was brief and he was allowed to return to Cyprus in 1957.

Greece applied in 1957 and 1958 to the United Nations to grant the right to self-government. The Turkish Cypriot minority, had not been considered of any importance by the Greek Cypriot majority in their plans for the future of the island, which resulted in Turkey calling for partition of the island.

An eventual solution was formulated in the Treaty of Zurich, by which time Grivas and his EOKA rebels had conducted a mission of massacre and terror resulting in a death toll in excess of 500.

The London Accord granting independence to Cyprus was signed on 19th February 1959 by Makarios, Dr Fazil Küçük (on behalf of the Turkish Cypriot Community), and the Prime Ministers of Great Britain, Greece and Turkey. The agreement was constructed in such a way as to provide safeguards protecting the minority Turkish Cypriot community, including powers of intervention to Britain, Turkey and Greece.

The truth obscured

The Republic of Cyprus became an actuality in August 1960, also joining the United Nations and the British Commonwealth. So much propaganda has been written about the Cyprus problem that at times it becomes very difficult to separate fact from fabrication. In particular the period from independence in 1960 to the Turkish armed forces intervention of 1974, has suffered from distorted half-truths being spread by the media.

The simple facts are thus: the constitution provided for a Greek President and Turkish Vice President, each with supposed powers to veto government decisions. This in fact did not happen because of the majority being firmly in favour of the Greeks. The civil service also employed a majority of Greeks. The balance in government and civil service being seventy to thirty per cent, armed forces and police sixty to forty per cent. There was no agreed structure for the army and Makarios decided there should be no armed forces on Cyprus. The legislation vote in the Cyprus House of Representatives required separate majorities from the Greek and Turkish members and the system proved unwieldy and impossible to administer effectively because an honest, simple democracy with majority rule would have had the end result of no voice for the Turkish people.

Towards the end of 1963 Grivas strengthened his pursuit of Enosis and heavily criticised Makarios and his government, provoking the EOKA rebels into action which he hoped would achieve the ultimate goal of complete union with Greece. Just before Christmas 1963 (it must be remembered that Christmas is the most important of the Christian festivals, celebrating as it does, the birth of Christ who came into the world to save it from evil), armed Greeks made a foray into the mostly Turkish suburb of Omorphita (now Kücük Kaymakli) in Nicosia (Lefkoşa) and opened fire on the Turkish inhabitants. They killed, captured and then tortured anyone who could not escape. This included the old, children and women.

The Turkish people took up arms to defend themselves and formed enclaves in which they could be as secure as possible.

The British set up a buffer zone dividing the city but this attempt to keep the two sides apart proved largely unsuccessful.

In March 1964 the UN troops took over with no better result. Makarios had renounced the conditions of the London Accord making it clear that he intended to pursue the cause of total self rule for Greek Cypriots which would end almost certainly with Enosis. Considerable pressure was applied by the other two guarantor powers with the result that Makarios withdrew his announcement in a radio broadcast. It made little difference, as the Greeks continued in their attempts to crush and exterminate the Turks. If they couldn't kill them then they would blockade the enclaves and cut off their supplies resulting in widespread hardship.

Continuing armed conflict forced Turkey to threaten military reprisal which was stalled by the military coup in Greece. Now Enosis suddenly became less attractive. There followed a sharp increase in the economy of Cyprus as the island became a favourite holiday destination and the building of new hotels and the development of seaside resorts underwent a major boost.

Grivas returned to Cyprus in 1974 with the intention of heading the armed forces and EOKA-B, but died suddenly of a heart attack. Makarios was re-elected as President after he renounced the call for Enosis and demanded the withdrawal of mainland Greek officers. This provoked the National Guards into storming the Presidential Palace in Nicosia. Makarios escaped the attempted military coup, which had been supported by the *junta* in Greece, and Turkey felt it had the right to intervene to prevent further bloodshed.

The country divides

Turkish forces landed on the island on 20th July 1974 and took over forty per cent of the island. In the diaspora that followed, approximately 150,000 Greeks moved south and 50,000 Turks moved into the north. The Turkish armed forces remained in the north, as they still do, and as in 1571 there was an influx of mainland Turks. Mostly farmers from Anatolia who were desperately needed to ensure a continuance of successful agricultural activities.

The founding of the TRNC in 1983 created a state that is unrecognised by any other country except Turkey. The states of Europe continue to impose great restrictions on trade with Northern Cyprus, refusing to accept produce until it has passed through Turkey and been repackaged. This reluctance on the part of Europe to trade one way with Northern Cyprus presents a strange, unjust dichotomy when it is very evident that manufacturers from all the EU countries are only too happy to *sell* their products to the north.

Relations between the two communities still remain at a stalemate, despite frequent attempts at negotiation to resolve the situation. No short-term measure would prove effective and the continuance of two separate states, recognised or not, at least ensures peace for the inhabitants. At the same time, the economic infrastructure continues to grow and benefit from the introduction of modern methods of farming and the rise in tourism – benefits that can only do good, and bring prosperity to Northern Cyprus.

FLORA & FAUNA

Wildlife

Since farming is not especially intensive in Northern Cyprus, wildlife can often live in harmony with agriculture. The variety of wild animals in Cyprus is low.

Mammals

Foxes and hares play in the cool of the evening and hedgehogs are common. The Cyprus hedgehog, probably introduced from South Africa, has one distinguishing feature which makes it plainly different from the common European hedgehog – it has extremely long ears.

There is an indigenous species of cow that is bred at a Government-run farm in Çatalköy. The Cyprus moufflon is an ancestor of the modern day sheep. Sadly it was hunted almost to the point of extinction and now survives, in small numbers, in the Paphos forest in the south.

Butterflies and snails

Butterflies, like the cleopatra and swallowtail, visit the flowers and where the strawberry tree is present as a larval food plant, the two-tailed pasha glides through the air.

Springtime is the best time to observe the butterflies when as many as fifty different migrant species pass through.

Many species of snail go into a form of summer hibernation known as aestivation and large clumps of them adorn the stems of plants.

Snakes

The snakes have the Kyrenia mountain range as their playground, hibernating during the winter, the warm days of spring and summer find them in the long grass, or basking on a wall in the sun. Most species are harmless and will quickly slither off when they are aware of someone approaching.

Visitors should be aware of:

The montpelier snake: likes to hide among the ruins, the bite can cause painful swellings and a headache.

The blunt-nosed viper: the end of its tail is yellow and hornlike. The bite is highly dangerous and medical attention is needed immediately.

The very long **black snake**, which has a silver underbelly, is totally harmless except to venomous snakes. The black snake was introduced to the island when the poisonous snakes became too numerous. The black snake is extremely efficient at controlling the population of the toxic variety and there are more beneficial than dangerous snakes to be seen.

Lizards

Tiny lizards frolic in the summer sunshine and are extremely entertaining as they jump and roll about in courtship or territorial combat. When attacked by a larger creature such as cat, dog or bird of prey, they have the ability to shed their tails, thus hopefully fooling the attacker and making a quick getaway.

The ancient ruins are home to a variety of larger lizards including the iguana-like dragon lizard; these will scuttle away rapidly when disturbed. They are mostly shy creatures and choose under-populated sites as their habitat.

Chameleon on a citrus tree branch

Chameleons are to be seen among garden trees and rock crevices. Their colour will adapt to suit their surroundings and they tend to be very slow moving creatures. Due to this slothfulness they fall prey to domestic pets and it is not unusual for a cat to present its owner with a chameleon!

Insects

The cicada is the noisiest insect that the visitor will encounter. It is diurnal and the mating call of the male is extremely intrusive. From approximately 9pm to 5am they sleep. The life span of the mature insect is only four to six weeks, at the end of which time the female will have mated and laid her eggs in the bark of young trees. When the egg hatches the grub contained therein will drop to the ground and burrow under the tree where it will attach itself to the roots and live off the sap for two to seventeen years.

The life cycle depends very much on the type of cicada and the latitude at which it is born. It will emerge eventually as a shelled six-legged creature which will climb onto an upright surface and then split open to hatch the perfect winged mature cicada.

And the survival process starts all over again.

Birdlife

Cyprus serves as a staging post for migrating birds flying between Europe and the Nile delta. Hundreds of thousands of birds pass through the island in spring and autumn.

Overgrown orchards and olive groves are the haunt of little owls, which nest in cracks and holes in the trees. Endemic Cyprus warblers, considered by some to be a relative of the widespread Sardinian warbler, can be seen searching for insects.

The overhead wires serve as ideal lookouts for red-footed falcons. Bee-eaters and rollers also survey the terrain for insect quarry, while buntings use the wires as song perches to advertise their territories. The quails' 'wet-my-lips' call is often the only clue as to their whereabouts.

In the autumn and winter the seeds provide food for larks and house sparrows, sometimes including the Spanish sparrow. Bare fields are the haunt of hooded crows and magpies. The lists of birds given at the various sites are only a guide and not definitive.

Watching sites

Koruçam Burnu

Situated north-west of **Sadrazamköy** village, the area between the village and the cape is a mixture of grassland with small strips of farmland. The road to Sadrazamköy is good, however from there to the cape it is in a bad condition and sometimes not passable by car. This is a good area in the spring and offers many interesting species:

Marsh harrier, sparrow hawk, quail, stone-curlew, bee-eater, hoopoe, wagtail, whinchat, isabelline, northern and black-eared wheatear, red-backed and woodchat shrike and Cretzschmar's bunting.

Geçitköy Reservoir

The reservoir was completed in 1989 and has become a valuable stopover site for migrants. It is next to the main Girne-Güzelyurt road and easily accessible from the main road south of **Geçitköy**. Because the water supply is permanent, bird watching is possible all year round.

Many different species of waterbirds have been seen here including bittern, squacco and purple herons, shoveller, pochard, and little crake.

In the surrounding grasslands: great spotted cuckoo, northern wheatear, bee-eater, roller, bonelli and wood warbler.

In winter: white wagtail, stonechat, robin and thrush. Breeding birds include little owl, Cyprus pied wheatear, cetti's fan-tailed and Cyprus warbler. To the north-east of the reservoir is Kornos Peak; griffon vulture and osprey can be observed flying here.

Gönyeli and Kanlıköy Reservoirs

Both reservoirs are north-west of Lefkoşa. **Kanlıköy**, the largest, is easily reached by following the road north from Kanlıköy village to the dam. **Gönyeli** is tricky to find. Leave Gönyeli northwards travelling up-hill past a Mercedes showroom on the right. At the crest of the hill, turn right onto a narrow road, left immediately, then sharp right onto a dirt track. The track leads down to the dam.

Excluding the very hot summer months of June, July and August the reservoirs provide good bird watch-ing all year round and more than 110 bird species have been seen at the two sites. Kanlıköy is a quiet area, whereas Gönyeli is popular at the weekends for picnickers and fishermen.

If the water supply lasts until September, Kanlıköy becomes an excellent site for migrating waders and herons including squacco heron, little egret, avocet, green-shank and sandpiper.

Gülseren and Glapsides wetlands

The **Glapsides** wetlands are near Gazimağusa, between the two junc-tions leading to the village of **Tuzla**. There are several different tracks off the main road down to these wetlands.

Gülseren is on the northern edge of Gazimağusa. Unfortunately most of the site lies within the Gülseren military camp. It is forbidden to take photographs or videos here. Do not attempt to enter the area from the coast. If there is water here, it is excellent for waders, herons, gulls and terns.

Glapsides is important for ducks, herons, waders and many species of gulls. Spring migration brings kingfisher, black-necked grebe, gadwell, shoveller, garganey, pallid, hen and marsh harrier, osprey and spur-winged plover.

The land between the floodlands includes the forest of Salamis. This often holds large numbers of great spotted cuckoo, bee-eater, roller, spotted and pied flycatcher, golden oriole and red-backed shrike. Resi-dent breeders in the area include barn owl, spectacled warbler and black francolin.

Lake Mehmetcik

A shallow, natural, seasonal lake which lies west-south-west of **Mehmetcik** in the Karpas Peninsula. The lake is visible on the left shortly before you arrive at the village. The migrant visitors here are: little bittern, glossy ibis, garganey, pin-tail, little stint, curlew, sandpiper, spotted redshank and greenshank. The surrounding area attracts many songbirds throughout the winter.

The Karpas Peninsula

The under-developed peninsula offers many attractions to migrating birds, and the number of species during both seasons is high. Various larks, wagtails, warblers and raptors are easy to spot. At **Zafer Burnu**, the cape beyond St Andreas, is an ex-cellent site for visible migration. In the spring you can see the passage of falcons, harriers and buzzards.

There are official shooting seasons for the game birds. The KKKKD is the Northern Cyprus society for the protection of birds and nature (KUŞKOR). They have a small but loyal membership. For further information please contact them at:

> PO Box 634
> Girne
> Mersin. 10
> Turkey
> ☎ 815 7337

The flora of Cyprus is various enough to please every-one, from the visitor who just wants to see valleys full of anemones to the serious botanist who would like to identify 400 plus specimens during their couple of weeks stay.

Undoubtedly spring is the time for anyone who wants to see the most prolific colour and greatest variety. Late February through to the end of April are the best months and even then flower availability will be subject to the rainfall (or lack of it) and temperature. Excessive heat in April can bring about an early end to the flowering period of several species particularly the anemones.

Wildflowers

However, there are wildflowers that continue flowering well into May and June. Among these are the monk's cowl or friar's cowl (*arisarum vulgare*)

the endlessly abundant yellow oxalis (*oxalis pes-caprae*) which is an agricultural nuisance growing in the orchards and arable fields. The verges and hillsides are awash with colour from the wild cistus (rock rose) that flowers from January to June.

The sage leafed rock rose (*cistus salviifolius*) is white with a yellow centre, the flower somewhat resembling a lightly poached egg, and when not in bloom the bushes look like wild sage, hence its Latin name. The taurus rock rose (*cistus creticus tauricus*) is a deep purple/pink, papery thin petaled flower with a much darker leaf and the pink rock rose (*cistus creticus parvifolius*) has a quite dark pink flower and greyish green leaf. Like the *cistus salviifolius*, these latter two types also have bright yellow stamens at their centre.

Asphodels

The two asphodel plants that grow here are the very common *asphodelus aestivus* which grows everywhere in any type of ground from sea level to mountain top, and the small and delicate, much rarer hollow stemmed asphodel (*asphodelus fistulosus*). The former makes its presence known by its strong

(cont'd overleaf)

Above: Crab spider devouring a bee on a wild orchid
Opposite: Turban buttercup (ranunculus asiaticus) at St Hilarion

and pungent aroma, which smells strongly of cat's urine. It may be because of this rather unpleasant smell that the plant is inedible among livestock. The latter plant is not so easily found but can be seen at **Othello's Tower** in Gazimağusa growing in the courtyard, the south-west tower and on top of the citadel walls.

Both asphodels have white flowers growing in a conical spear at the top of tall straight stems, the *asphodelus aestivus* growing to a height of 40 inches (1m) and the *asphodelus fistulosus* grows to approximately 6 inches (15cm). The leaves of the former are lancelike and of the latter hollow like the culinary chive.

Autumn

Come the late summer and into early autumn, few flowers can survive the burning heat, but the solitary tall stem, topped with a white spear of flowers that seemingly grow straight out of the bare earth is that of the sea squill (*urginea maritime*). The broad almost flat strap-like leaves appear in spring from the bulb underground and these die back before the single flower stem comes into bloom. The bulbs of this plant have been used since Pliny's time for the manufacture of medicine to treat such diverse ailments as coughs and heart disease.

From September onwards the autumn flowers start to appear. The Cyprus cyclamen, (*cyclamen cyprium*) which will continue flowering until the end of January, can be found among the trees near the mountain castles. Usually it prefers a shady habitat. The autumn squill (*scilla autumnalis*), which grows from a leafless bulb until flowering has finished, has a stem, approximately 2.75 inches (7cm), that produces a small cluster of pink/violet flowers. It likes a dry habitat and rocky hillsides. The romulea (*romulea tempskyana*) resembles a small crocus, it grows from a corm and has dark purple petals with an orange centre. They have a fairly varied habitat and therefore are widespread, certainly among the hillsides of the Beşparmak mountains and on the roadsides all along the forest tracks. It can be seen from December to April.

Spring

Real spring colour comes with a profusion of the yellow flowering plants which can be seen everywhere. The first hint of spring sunshine is produced by the oxalis, seen in the olive groves and the citrus orchards, and in any flowerbed that has not been kept weedfree during winter.

Anemones

Then come the anemones (*anemone coronaria*) and a swathe of these flowers in every colour from white to pink, to red, to darkest purple, is one of the most remarkable and memorable sights to behold. One of the best places to see this is in the valley on the southern side of the Five Finger (Beşparmak) Mountain.

Mandrake

The beautiful mandrake (*mandragora officinarium*) has a widespread habitat and can be easily found beside the paths that wind upwards through St Hilarion Castle and on waste ground and roadsides. Instantly recognised by its low-to-the-ground growth of broad leaves which are coarse and have a strong central rib. From the rosette of leaves grows a cluster of blue to purple flowers, which turn into an orange ovoid fruit. (This is not edible and should be avoided, as the mandrake is one of the many poisonous plants that grow on Cyprus).

Crown daisy

Vast expanses of very dark yellow proclaim the presence of the crown daisy (*chrysanthemum coronarium*) growing on the roadsides, waste ground and at most of the historical sites. Intermingling with the wild chrysanthemum will be found the field marigold (*calendula arvensis*), scabious (*scabiosa prolifera*) with its multiple branches bearing creamy-white flowers that look like small pincushions, and the tassel hyacinth (*muscari comosum*) not to be confused with the similar grape hyacinth (*bellevalia trifoliata*).

Everlasting sungold

Growing more on waste ground and very barren land will be found the everlasting sungold (*helichrysum conglobatum*), which like many of the *helichrysum* family retains its wonderful colour for months, and the rather unattractively named grecian fleabane (*phagnalon rupestra*).

Anchusa

Providing splashes of blue on the roadsides and on dry hills, the stately, feathery leafed anchusa (*anchusa azurea*) and the very much smaller, more attractive dark-blue of the *anchusa undulata*. It is easy at first glance to confuse the *anchusa azurea* with the Cyprus viper bugloss (*echuim plantageneum*) though looking more closely it will be seen that the blue flower of the bugloss is more bell-like in shape.

Ranunculus

There are beautiful ranunculus to be seen flowering from February to May on the hillsides of the Beşparmak range. The turban buttercup and Persian crowfoot (*ranunculus asiaticus*) grow in a variety of colours from pale cream to yellow; white flashed with red and deep dark scarlet. These are not to be confused with anemones which will be found in the same habitat.

(cont'd overleaf)

(cont'd from previous page)

Giant fennel

The giant fennel (*ferula communis*) is another of those plants inedible to man or beast and therefore grows rampantly unchecked. It is unmissable, as the flower stems topped with many heads of bright yellow flowers grow to a height in excess of 6.5 feet (2m). Local florists use the feathery leaf in their flower arrangements and in ancient time the dry stems were used as tinder.

Black tulip & corn flag

Less easy to find is the black tulip (*tulipa cypria*) not truly black but very, very dark red and to be found mostly in cornfields where it dwells side by side with the common corn flag (*gladiolus italicus*) a pink wild gladioli which the local children will pick and sell in bunches at the roadside.

Arabian & Cyprus sun roses

Two yellow flowers both with papery thin petals which often grow together and are sometimes mistaken one for the other are the Arabian sun rose (*fumana arabica*) and the yellow Cyprus sun rose (endemic) (*helianthemum obtusifoluim*). They favour the same habitat of dry rocky places and flower from February to May.

The flowers described here are only a sample of the specimens to be found on Cyprus and most of them are described more fully and accompanied by excellent colour photographs in *The Flowers of Northern Cyprus* by Sonia Halliday and Laura Lushington. This pocket-sized book is available from The Green Jacket Bookshop in Girne.

FOOD & DRINK

Cypriot cuisine is a wonderful mix of the Eastern Mediterranean and has many characteristics taken from the island's numerous conquerors. It will not take long for the tourist to discover why one of the national pastimes is eating. A most memorable part of any holiday will be missed if the local cuisine is not sampled.

Cypriots are ingenious cooks, using raw materials which would not occur to anyone else. An example of this is *gabbar*, wild caper. The plant grows freely on the dry slopes all over Cyprus. The unopened flower buds and tender stem tops are pickled in vinegar and eaten as part of the *Meze*.

'Meze' is the Turkish word for hors-d'oeuvres. In many of the village restaurants food will start arriving on the table soon after you sit down; this means that there is a set menu and these will be the meze 'starters'. Most of the appetisers will have been grown or made locally and will change seasonally.

Remember that this is only the

Orchids

The orchids start to appear towards the end of December from the brown bee orchid (*ophrys fusca*), and the green winged orchid (*orchis morio*) which can be found among the pine forests, to the pyramidal orchid (*anacamptis pyramidalis*) which flowers March to May. The latter also has a habitat among pine woods and dry grassy places.

Orchid types to be found include: the ploughshare orchid (*serapias vomeracea*); eastern woodcock orchid (*ophrys umbilicata*); naked man orchid (*orchis italica*). All the above are fairly widespread and have a flowering season from February to May.

The naval orchid is one of the many different bee orchids that can be found in Northern Cyprus

beginning of a Turkish meal so *'yavaş yavaş'* (slowly slowly).

Cypriots are great meat eaters, using lamb and chicken in their cooking. All the meat is locally reared. There is no import licence issued for fresh meat. As they are Muslim, pork is not used.

Meze, a meal in itself

Expect to receive up to fifteen small dishes of food including the delicious yoghurt, rice, stuffed vegetables, black-eyed beans, hummous (puree of chickpeas and sesame paste) and *nor* (white cheese).

As these are slowly savoured a selection of hot starters will be served such as *sigara börek* (cheese-filled filo pastry), *köfte* (spicy meatball) and the tasty *hellim* cheese. Be sure to squeeze the juicy fresh lemon over the food, especially the kebabs.

Main courses normally include *şiş kebab* (chunks of lamb or chicken on the skewer), lamb chops, grilled chicken, *şeftali kebab* (Turkish sausage) or fish. When coming to a Mediterranean island, fish is expected to be found in abundance. However, as with so many other places, the seas have been over-fished. For the best selection go to a specialist fish restaurant and ask what the 'catch of the day' is. Grouper, red mullet, sea bream and sea bass are popular. *Local tip*, don't eat fish if the sea has been rough and the boats have not been out. It will be frozen, or left over from the previous day!

Main courses are served with salad and chips. Please do not think that it is only the tourists who are served chips. Everyone loves chips and when they are made from the delicious Cypriot potatoes they are irresistible. Sometimes the chips are put on the table as the meze is being eaten. Don't be too shy to ask the waiter to serve them with the main course. Most waiters are very obliging.

After this feast there is not normally room left for dessert. Many of the restaurants will serve a plate of seasonal fruits. Cypriots have a very sweet palate and enjoy sticky, gooey desserts like *baklava* (pastry with nuts and syrup).

Restaurants

Northern Cyprus has an abundance of restaurants offering a wealth of culinary choice. Between Girne and Güzelyurt there are some 350 establishments, serving French, Chinese, Indian, European and even Irish cuisine. Most hotels have a restaurant but it is better to go out and eat as the quality of food and atmosphere

is better. Be adventurous, some of the ragged looking establishments can surprise you with the quality of food on offer. Weekends are normally busy, the whole family, from toddler to grandmother get together and eat at their favourite restaurant. Cypriots tend to eat late, especially in the heat of the summer.

Wines

Wine making in the north is still in its infancy so the Turkish mainland wines are preferred. A good selection of white and red wine will be found in even small restaurants. Some of the international establishments also stock well known French, German and Italian wines.

Turkish wines	
Çankaya	white, very dry
Efsane	white, fruity, dry
Villa Doluca	white, exceedingly drinkable, dry
Nevsah	white, easy to drink, dry
Villa Doluca	red, smooth and rich
Yakut	red, good quality, dry
Dikmen	red, light, easy drinking
Külüp Özel Reserve	red, dry and robust
Lâl	rosé, medium and light

Zıvanıa – Cyprus Whisky

Zıvania is a very strong, domestic made spirit often referred to as fire water! It is made from the left-overs after wine making is finished.

The *kazan*, a copper pot, is filled with a fermented mess of grape remains and water. A fire is made and the pot is placed on top. A condenser is attached to the kazan with tubes and in turn the tubes lead to a bottle. The water in the condenser is continually replaced to keep it cool, a bucketful out and another in. The resulting alcohol falls into the waiting bottle. It is a very slow process, but in eight hours time what was originally a ton of grapes is now several bottles of Zivania. When the mixture inside begins to dry it is removed, and the goats get the remnants of the remains for dessert!

The Zivania is run through the still again to remove impurities. With grapes or potatoes the result is almost pure alcohol and quite tasteless. To add a flavour Cypriots add such things as basil and fig seeds. The old village custom is to down a gulp on cold mornings, or enjoy a small measure with your meal. It is also used to soothe muscular aches and pains and even as a cleaning agent. However, there is always some available in the home to demonstrate the strength of 'Cyprus Whisky' to visitors from abroad.

Other drinks

The national drink, Brandy Sour, makes a delicious aperitif. It consists of a generous helping of local brandy with bitters, lemon squash (usually home made) and soda.

Rakı is the Turkish equivalent of Pernod. Known as 'lion's milk', the aniseed spirit turns cloudy when diluted with water. It makes a good accompaniment to a fish meze and at £1.50 a bottle is very good value!

The Safa brewery in Gazimağusa makes Gold Fassl, a light lager beer and the popular Efes lager is imported from Turkey. Most international liqueurs are on sale.

For non-alcoholic drinks be sure to try fresh orange juice, homemade lemonade (*lemonarta*), and *Ayran*. Ayran is yoghurt diluted with water, slightly salted with mint on the top. It cools down the body temperature and can help settle upset stomachs.

Turkish coffee

Once a delicacy of the Ottoman upper classes, Turkish coffee is now enjoyed by all. The secret of Turkish coffee is to use good coffee beans and to create froth on the top. It is served in small cups in four different ways:

Sade	without sugar
As Şekerli	with a little sugar
Orta	medium sugar
Şekerli	with *lots* of sugar

If trying Turkish coffee for the first time choose Orta. Even if sugar is not normally taken in beverages, most tourists enjoy this variety. Normally a glass of water will be served with the coffee.

There is a lovely old story behind this tradition. Every day Mustafa would get up and take himself off to the village coffee shop. There he would sit for the day chatting with his friends and playing backgammon. Ayşen his wife was most upset by

(cont'd on page 44)

The Selemiye Mosque (St Sophia) in Lefkoşa

Recipe for Molohiya

Many people are intrigued with this local dish made using molohiya, a spinach-like plant, and are keen to know how it is prepared.

- 2lbs (1kg) chicken joints or same weight of lamb pieces
- 5.5lbs (2.5kg) molohiya
- 2 onions
- 4 garlic cloves
- 1 tin of chopped tomatoes
- 1 tbsp tomato paste
- local olive oil
- 30.5 fluid ozs (900ml) chicken stock
- Plenty of fresh lemon juice

Unless the dish is being prepared when the molohiya is in season, dried molohiya is used. This should be soaked overnight in cold water.

Heat the oil in a large saucepan and fry the meat until golden brown on both sides. Remove the meat and put the finely sliced onions and roughly chopped garlic in the pan. Sweat these until soft.

Return the meat to the pan and add the chopped tomatoes, tomato paste and hot chicken stock. Season well.

After washing and draining the molohiya add to the pan with some lemon juice and bring to the boil. Cover the pan and leave to simmer gently for 1-2 hours or until the meat is deliciously tender. Serve with soft chunky cut bread, fresh onions and lots of lemon juice.

Above: A shepherd and his flock on the Mesaoria plain
Below: The partially rebuilt theatre at Soli

Cypriot food

Bumbar	sausage made with lamb mince and rice
Çakıstes	crushed green olives
Ekmek kadayıfı	syrup-soaked sponge
Firin kebab	normally lamb, cooked very slowly in the clay oven with a bay leaf and potatoes
Hellim cheese	locally produced from goats milk, delicious fried or grilled
Katmer	filo pastry with nuts
Kolokas	similar to a yam, used instead of potatoes in dishes like moussaka
Marcon	unripe walnuts preserved in a thick syrup
Molohiya	a plant rather like spinach, cooked as a stew with chicken or lamb and plenty of tomatoes, garlic and lemon juice
Stuffed artichokes	the head of the plant is stuffed with minced meat and rice
Tava	casserole with lamb and cumin
Tuzlu Balik	a large fish, covered in rock salt and baked in the oven

this and one day decided to poison him.

His friend Ali heard of the plot and warned Mustafa. When the poisoned coffee was served to Mustafa he asked for a glass of water. He poured some of the cold water into his coffee knowing that if there were any poison in the cup it would rise to the top. A lot of men still pour some cold water into their coffee before drinking!

If 'normal' coffee is required remember to ask for 'Nescafé'.

Unfortunately Turkish çay (tea) is quite difficult to come by, as many Cypriots prefer English-style tea with milk.

CLIMATE

The climate is equable and rarely, except upon the mountain tops, does the temperature drop to freezing. Snow is so rare that in February 1997, when a heavy snowstorm covered villages in the mountain foothills, the children stared in wide eyed amazement at the remarkable phenomenon and were given a day off school to enjoy the fun of snow fights and building snowmen.

The summer is hot with the highest temperatures in July and August. It is also during these two months that the humidity is at its highest. For sun worshippers this is the time for relaxing around swimming pools (and most of the hotels have one) or swimming in the crystal clear sea.

THE PEOPLE

The Turkish Cypriot people are welcoming to an unexpected degree.

They are friendly, helpful and will invite the visitor into their home, not just for a glass of *çay* (tea), or cup of coffee, but will also share whatever food they may have. They have a courtesy rarely found elsewhere and delight in the company of new-found friends.

More than anything, Turkish Cypriots are warm hearted, fun loving people with a real sense of family loyalty. Don't be surprised if the hotel courtesy bus picks up children on their way home from school or a woman returning from shopping, carrying heavy bags. It is the kind of old fashioned courtesy that is now sadly lacking in the developed western world. Polite and helpful, Cypriots want you to enjoy your stay.

Historical life goes back to the seventh millennium BC. Throughout these years Cyprus has had foreign people on her soil, passing by or settling, leaving parts of their culture behind. Despite this the Cypriots have their own identity and will fiercely point out that they are not from the mainland (Turkey). They have a laid back attitude to life which makes for a most relaxing holiday. Visitors do not have to worry about being over-charged. This goes as far as the waiters who do not stand holding their hands out for a tip.

Language

Turkish is the predominant language, however Cypriots have their own version. Just as parts of England have adapted the English language so the Turkish Cypriots have their own words. *Napiyorsunuz* (What are you doing?) becomes 'Napan' amongst friends as they greet each other.

English is widely spoken and understood with many Cypriots having lived in England or with relatives residing there. Don't be surprised to be asked where you are from and for the locals to know your nearest pub or street! Enjoy the hospitality. It is quite common for a shopkeeper to offer you a coffee or cold drink. Etiquette says that it is not polite to leave before the coffee cup gets cold.

What does the future hold?

A popular pastime is reading the grains of Turkish coffee, which spread in all different shapes around the cup when it is turned upside down into the saucer after drinking. Each shape has a different meaning:

a ring	– marriage
dog	– you have a friend
birds	– messengers bringing news
water	– travel overseas or a visitor from abroad
snake	– an enemy

Religion

The religion is Muslim but most Cypriots do not practise their faith. There are very few covered women here and those that are will be from Turkey. After 1974 the Turkish Cypriot government invited Turkish people to settle in the under-populated North. They needed help with industry and agriculture. Many of these people have made Cyprus their home. The call to prayer is made five times a day. Strict Muslims do not drink or gamble.

1 Girne (Kyrenia)

Girne has for years been the showpiece of Cyprus. Long before partition, both foreign and local tourists would flock to this very pretty town with its small and ancient harbour. Here they could take advantage of the cooling breeze blowing in from the sea, sit outside one of the cafés that form the background of the harbour promenade and sip a cold beer or refreshing brandy sour.

HISTORY

Founded probably in the tenth century BC by the early settlers, Girne became one of the major city kingdoms. Because of its position on the northern shore, at approximately halfway from west to east, it became a natural point to develop a harbour and is only a short distance from Turkey, a journey easily covered by sailing craft of ancient times.

There is little recorded history of the town's early development and nothing of any note until Byzantine rule when the town was fortified against the Arab raids of the seventh century.

The Lusignans developed the town and strengthened the **castle** which they used as a royal residence as well as a military fort. So strongly did they re-fortify it, that when the Genoese overran the island in 1373/74 the castle effectively withstood the siege.

The Venetians strengthened the castle in 1544, placing the new huge walls and towers outside the old castle perimeter and adding two strong landward bastions and one seaward to protect the harbour entrance.

Despite these efforts against attack, when the Ottomans struck in 1570 they encountered no resistance. Girne, already apprised of the massacre that had taken place in Nicosia, felt that the might of the Ottoman army was not to be thwarted and capitulated without firing a single shot.

Under the Ottomans the town was simply a minor port and the population, through lack of enterprise and employment, dwindled.

When the British took over as governors of the island, they found the town with its quiet sleepy

• Shopping

Although Northern Cyprus is certainly not a 'shopping Mecca' there are certain items you may be tempted by. Girne and Lefkoşa have the best selection of shops. Negotiating or 'haggling' is not something that most shopkeepers get involved with. If you have sterling cash with you, then try your luck but if your offer is refused that is the final word. The owner will not come running after you like in Turkey!

Most visitors to Cyprus look forward to purchasing a bottle or two of their favourite liquor. Popular brand cigarettes can also be purchased at discounted prices. The best price is from the duty free shops at Ercan Airport. Remember to check the customs allowance.

The White Dove's statue marks the beginning of Girne high street. You will find everything from grocers, to jewellers and boutiques.

Fake designer clothes are an excellent buy. The quality and price tends to differ from shop to shop so have a good look around.

If spectacles or sunglasses are on your shopping list, try **Akay Optik** in the high street on the right. They stock all the leading brands and will make up prescription lenses. Arranging an eye test is easy. Call **Dr Deniz** on ☎ 815 4950.

Gold and silver are in abundance. The designs are most unusual and prices are reasonable. The cost is calculated on the weight of the article. Look out for the beautiful Ottoman wall mirrors, made of solid silver. **Erdal's** jewellery shop (turn right at the main crossroads heading towards the harbour) has many lovely pieces. Copy watches are a popular present. A Gucci or Rolex only costs about £10.00 sterling.

For a really good bric-a-brac shop go to **The Old Bazaar**. Situated along the sea wall just before the harbour entrance,

atmosphere appealing, and began to develop it slowly as an ideal place for gentle recreation. They also made use of the excellent facilities of the castle and developed a prison and police academy within it.

The **Dome Hotel** was built to accommodate visitors and for many years was the only hotel in Girne. When it opened in 1939 the single storey building was surmounted by a dome, hence the name.

in Girne •

there is an amazing collection of Turkish pottery, tiles, silk cushion covers, scarves and ornaments of all descriptions. Don't forget to buy a **'Nazar'** or evil eye to ward off the evil spirits.

On the edge of Girne, before The Jasmine Court Hotel is the **Green Jacket Bookshop**. Here you will find maps, postcards, paintings, a wide selection of guidebooks and some local handicrafts.

Continuing west along the same road is **Dizayn 74** (although not within walking distance). All the pottery is made and hand painted on the premises.

Cash

There are many banks throughout Girne, however it is quicker and easier to use the exchange bureaux for obtaining cash. Cashpoint machines are situated at **İş Bankasi**, on the corner of Atatürk Caddesi and **Vakıflar Bankasi**, on Ecevit Caddesi, near the small roundabout.

These machines accept credit cards that display the international visa sign. After inserting the card you will be asked what language you require. The machines only use Turkish Lira. All of the shops will be delighted to deal in sterling and will give you change in TL.

Chemists and drug stores

Many pharmacists speak good English and can give medical advice over the counter. One of the better-stocked chemists (*eczane* in Turkish) is **Enver**, which is found in Girne high street opposite The Bristol Hotel. Generally open from 8.30am-6pm Monday to Friday.

The chemists operate a rota system ensuring one chemist is open 24 hours and on Sundays. The duty chemist is advertised in *The Cyprus Today* newspaper and in the window of the other chemists.

However as the town became more popular and the need for hotel accommodation increased, the dome was removed to allow the addition of more rooms on the first floor. The name remained the same and through the following decades the Dome has become larger. There is now a casino to cater for the gamblers and most recently the building of a fresh-water swimming pool.

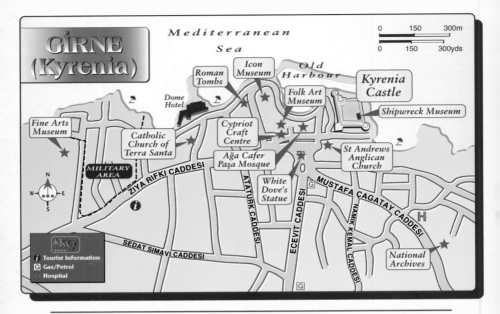

PLACES TO SEE

From the harbour it is only a short walk to visit some of the major attractions of the town.

Apart from **Kyrenia Castle** which also houses the fascinating **Shipwreck Museum**, (a must on the visitor's list), other places of interest and all within walking distance of the town centre include: the **Icon Museum** in the Archangel Michael church; the **rock cut tombs** which can be seen just across the street from the Icon Museum and are situated underneath the **Perge Café**; the **Folk Art Museum** in the harbour and the **Cypriot Craft Centre** situated in one of the round towers of the **old city walls** off the main street (Ziya Rifki Caddesi) on the seaward side.

The old harbour

The picturesque old harbour is mostly lined with long-disused carob warehouses. These have now undergone tasteful remodelling and have been turned into flats, bars, cafés and restaurants. There are plenty of good local places to eat, in fact so many, that choosing where to go is one of the most difficult decisions that the holidaymaker has to face. The best value will always be the restaurants that specialise in local food. Prices in the old harbour tend to be slightly higher than in the villages but it is a small price to pay for such a wonderful atmosphere. Beware of restaurants which are of an international style, they tend to charge about twice as much for their food and drinks.

Back streets

No visitor should miss a walk through the back streets. It is there they will find the real heart of the town and some of the 'best buys', hidden away in small shops that on entering suddenly become an Aladdin's cave stocked with a remarkable and eclectic selection.

(cont'd on page 56)

Above: Folk dancers in Kyrenia Harbour

Below: Kyrenia old harbour

• KYRENIA CASTLE •

History

Almost all of the external walls and towers date from the time of the Venetians. However behind these massive defences lies a complicated mixture of building styles from centuries before.

It is most probable that there was an early Roman fort protecting the trade going through Girne harbour and the Byzantines built on top of it. This structure was very much smaller than the present castle, consisting of a simple square with four towers, one on each corner. The castle was originally protected by a moat and had an inner harbour which connected to the outside via a sea gate in the north wall.

The Lusignans strengthened the castle walls and added the north-east tower as the new lookout point when they took over the island.

When the Venetians increased the castle walls, towers and bastions, they created a piece of military architecture, which can only compare with the Citadel in Gazimağusa for purpose-built strength against the might of enemy cannons.

The present day entrance is across a solid bridge through an arch that was once protected by a drawbridge. The entrance passage ascends a sharp incline and on the right there is a flight of stone steps, which lead down to the water gate.

Take care: the steps are uneven and the descent is unlit.

Touring the castle

On the left, up three steps there is a passageway leading to the twelfth century Byzantine **church of St George**. The chapel remained outside the castle walls and was used by the French rulers as the Catholic church for the town. This quite delightful little church has a central dome supported by four Corinthian columns made of white marble and the remnants of opus sectile (ornamentally patterned) flooring. The Venetians after erecting their walls outside the perimeter of the church then filled in the space surrounding it to create the north-west bastion and now all that remains visible is the domed roof.

There is no access to the castle from the church so it is necessary to retrace one's steps back to the main entrance passage. At the top of the entrance slope there is a large room which has an exhibition showing the various stages of the castle's development. The fourteenth century French **gatehouse** has the Lusignan coat of arms above the entrance and also evidence of the apparatus that pulled up the portcullis that protected this gate.

On entering the gateway the tomb of the Ottoman admiral Sadik Paşa is to be seen. He was one of the many commanding officers of the Ottoman forces who lost their lives during the conquest of Cyprus.

On entering the courtyard and turning right is the entrance to the **French dungeons**. The Antiquities Department have very enterprisingly created here a torture chamber, which is most entertaining if one's taste is for the grisly and macabre. Also in the 'oubliettes' are effigies of some people who in error upset members of the royal family. (King Peter's mistress Jeanne was imprisoned here by his wife the evil Queen Eleanor and John Visconti, imprisoned by King Peter because the King refused to believe John Visconti's tales of the queen's infidelity.)

To the left of the courtyard entrance, flights of steps lead up into **royal apartments** which had broad balconies looking out over the large square court.

Facing the sea, the crenellations on the **north wall** are the work of the French masons and have embrasures for the archers and arrow slits. The rooms built along the wall served as barracks, the British used some of them as prison cells and in the present day those on the ground floor are equipped to provide refreshments and souvenirs.

The **north-east tower** was unchanged by the Venetians and remains as built by the French. There are exhibitions in the two lofty rooms of this tower. One has reasonably lifelike effigies of soldiers through the ages who would have been billeted within the castle walls and the other contains the weapons of war used by successive inhabitants to protect their realm.

The **east wing** comprises a series of apartments which have been restored and lead into the section which now houses the **Shipwreck Museum**. This ship which was found by a local diver in 1965 was raised with great care by a recovery team from the University of Pennsylvania. After being brought up from the sea it was impregnated with preservatives and is now kept in a special air-conditioned chamber.

There is an exhibition of photographs from the recovery expedition on display and a cross-section reconstruction of what the original ship would have looked like.

There were personal utensils for four people implying that the ship had a four-man crew and as the vessel was found in less than 100ft (30m) of water and approximately a mile (1.6km) offshore there is all probability that the crew swam to safety.

The oldest ship ever found at sea

Estimated to have sunk circa 300BC and already eighty years old, the recovered hull in the shipwreck museum is, to date, the oldest ship ever to be recovered from the seabed. Made from Aleppo pine she is thought to have plied her trade along the coast of Asia Minor before crossing to Cyprus.

The cargo of amphorae, from Samos and Rhodes, and basalt mills from Cos was recovered almost intact. The amphorae contained almonds which have been carbon dated to 288BC plus or minus sixty years.

(cont'd overleaf)

• KYRENIA CASTLE •

Above: Kyrenia Castle, the upper walls from the north-east tower

Left: Ancient amphorae, grain mills and the ship reconstruction in the Shipwreck Museum

Below: The inner court showing the eastward apartments which contain the Shipwreck Museum

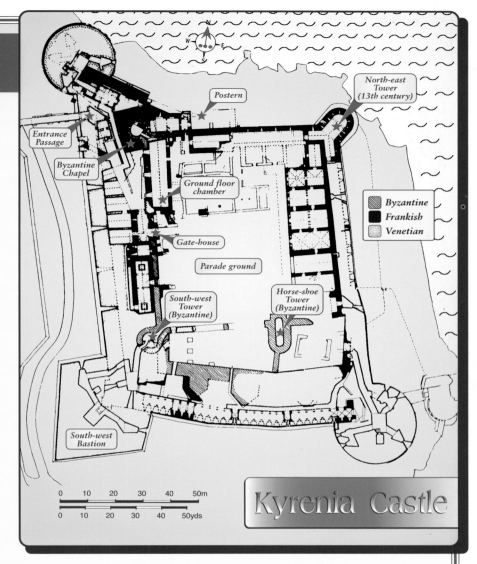

Kyrenia Castle

Map labels:

- Postern
- North-east Tower (13th century)
- Entrance Passage
- Byzantine Chapel
- Ground floor chamber
- Gate-house
- Parade ground
- South-west Tower (Byzantine)
- Horse-shoe Tower (Byzantine)
- South-west Bastion

Legend:
- Byzantine
- Frankish
- Venetian

Scale:
| 0 | 10 | 20 | 30 | 40 | 50m |
| 0 | 10 | 20 | 30 | 40 | 50yds |

On leaving the shipwreck exhibition hall, cross the courtyard to the south-west tower, originally of Byzantine construction and now firmly enclosed by the huge Venetian diamond-shaped bastion. There are positions for cannon on several levels but access is difficult.

Returning to the gatehouse entrance, instead of descending the passage for the castle exit, climb the ramp built by the Venetians, to enable them to draw their cannon and ammunition with relative ease, and the dome of the Byzantine church will come into view. On the far side of the dome the **north-west tower** is a vantage point not to be missed. The view across Girne harbour and of the castle of St Hilarion and the mountains is spectacular.

Churches

There are two churches that cater for the small Christian community. **St Andrews Anglican church** situated very close to the Police Station will welcome all denominations and has services every Sunday and on Holy Days.

The **Catholic Church of Terra Santa** (the Holy Ground) is in Ersin Sokak opposite the Dome Hotel. Mass is held on the first and third Sundays of the month at 12 noon. This strange church, which at first glance looks Byzantine, is in fact a twentieth century edifice built by two locals who felt that the Catholic minority should have their own church in which to worship. They used stone from old buildings and ruined churches as is evident if the masonry is studied carefully, and they modelled the building on the Greco-Byzantine style.

It is quite understandable that the church could be mistaken for something older except when one looks at the window frames and realises they are very much 1930s modern iron, going rusty. The church grounds are sadly untended and there is a general air of neglect, the Catholic population too few and too widespread to take care of them.

Folk Art Museum

The main entrance to the Folk Art Museum is from the promenade in the old harbour. Formally a granary, it was donated to the Antiquities Department by Lady Loch. It is a reconstruction of a typical Cypriot house displaying bridal costumes and a variety of needlework. On the ground floor is an olive press and a threshing board.

Ağa Cafér Paşa Mosque

The mosque behind the harbour was built by a Turkish landowner soon after 1580 and bears his name, Ağa Cafér Paşa Mosque. The mosque is well-sited; it not only overlooks the harbour, but is also close to an ancient spring, which was used for the ritual ablutions. The spring, with a stone fountain, is still in use today. The minaret is built of local stone and the Muezzin calls out the prayer or *'Ezan'* five times a day. It is sung in Arabic.

Church of Chrysopolitissa

The old Christian church of Chrysopolitissa is situated nearly opposite the rear entrance of the Folk Art Museum. Although roofless, the walled up Gothic archway is interesting. This building is being rented by the National Trust of Northern Cyprus (☎ 815 3738), who are trying to raise the funds to erect a new roof and eventually use the church as their headquarters. There are some 200 members, who have done much work in raising funds and organising tree planting after the terrible fire that raged for four days along the mountains in 1995.

Icon Museum

Peering over the western end of the harbour is the tower of Archangelos church, dedicated to the Archangel Michael; this is now an **Icon Museum**. The church was built at the end of the nineteenth century and opened as the Girne Icon Museum on 11th June 1990. The icons are a collection from the various Greek Orthodox churches in the surrounding area, it being safer to house them under one roof.

The conventions of iconography are rigidly stylised and therefore virtually unchanging. The methods still used today were established in the sixth century. An icon must not be a caricature, nor must there be any three-dimensional effect, the figure must appear flat. Prayers are said before the process begins so that the spirit of God is with the artist. The icon is venerated not for itself, but for what it represents.

Tombs

Opposite the church are some tombs that were hewn out of the limestone rock, these date back to about the fourth century.

Lusignan round tower

The old city of Girne was surrounded by walls, fortified by towers. The best preserved of these is off the high street. This Lusignan round tower has been carefully restored and is now used as a tasteful gift shop.

In & around the harbours

Walking towards the harbour from here the road follows the direction of the curtain wall along which other remnants may be identified. There is part of a **tower** on the left, in between houses, retaining its machicolations, or overhanging parapets. These contained slots down which stones, hot water etc, were poured onto an attacking enemy. The machicolations are supported by stone corbels.

The **small tower** in the harbour, which is commonly mistaken for an old lighthouse, stands at the entrance of the ancient harbour. This stone pedestal had a pillar on top, from which a heavy chain was slung across the port entrance and connected on the opposite side by the present Custom House. The chain would be raised when an enemy ship was approaching the port.

The **stone quay** is a relatively recent feature. There was a beach extending from the custom house to the castle, and rope and windlass hauled up the merchant sailing boats. The stone axle sockets can be seen on the walls between the Corner Restaurant and Marabou. The stone bollards dotted around the quayside were used to tie up the ships.

The main export was carob beans, which were in great demand for horse and cattle fodder. The sacks of beans would be brought in by cart to the upper floors of the warehouses, which were accessed from the narrow streets at the back, as they are on a higher level. This explains why the Folk Art Museum has an entrance off the back street.

The new harbour on the eastern edge of Girne is very much a working port. It is where the ferryboats go across to the Turkish mainland. For information on trips call ☎ 815 2344. The nearby site of **Chrysokava**, mentioned in so many guidebooks, is now, unfortunately, inaccessible.

Fine Arts Museum

Situated on the western edge of Girne the museum is worth a visit for the building itself, it was a villa built in the 1930s by a wealthy Briton. Situated near the military hospital it is marked as 'Güzel Sanatlar Muzesi' on the TO map. A collection of paintings, embroideries and porcelain is on display.

• BELLAPAIS VILLAGE

• BELLAPAIS VILLAGE

Getting there

The road eastwards from Girne branches right at a staggered cross-roads on the outskirts of town and at the next cross-roads go straight across. The road is signposted for Ozanköy and Beylerbeyi (Bellapais). The route travels through the **Altinkaya** holiday complex and a couple of hundred yards further on, the road to Bellapais branches to the right with **Ozanköy** (the Village of the Poets) straight ahead.

The road leading to Bellapais is lined on either side with imposing villas, some still under construction and all of them an outward demonstration of certain wealth. The modern housing contrasts sharply with the sorry state of dereliction to be found among the old Cypriot homes in the main village. Many of them were vacated by Greeks after 1974 and have now fallen into a state of total disrepair.

The road levels out just before entering the village itself, there is an army camp entrance to the right and a road leads ahead which takes the mountain route to the southern slopes of the Beşparmak range. (It is signposted **Ambelia Village** – built pre-1974 and the first purpose built holiday village in the north.)

Follow the road into the village passing a small white Orthodox church now converted to the village mosque on the left, and the centre of the village is soon reached. Parking is difficult and it is advisable to bear left at the 'Tree of Idleness', Huzur Ağaç restaurant, and continue to the rear of the abbey building to park, preferably in the shade of the huge carob tree which dominates the parking area.

History of the abbey

This abbey, also known as the White Abbey because of the white habits worn by the Premonstratensian order of monks, derives its name from the corruption of *Abbaye de la Pais*. The Abbey of Peace, and truly it is one of the most tranquil and serene places on the island, was founded at the beginning of the thirteenth century by the Augustinian order fleeing their erstwhile kingdom of Jerusalem.

Thierry, Archbishop of Cyprus persuaded them to adopt the rule that arose in Premontré in northern France. Under Thierry's guidance the abbey prospered and became influential, so much so that it was necessary for Pope Gregory IX in 1232 to remind the Abbot of his canonical obedience and spend less time on secular affairs of state.

In 1246 the abbey benefited from a large legacy bequeathed by a knight simply known as Roger the Norman and he also endowed them with a piece of the true cross.

& ABBEY •

To be the possessors of such a sacred relic made the abbey the focus of some very wealthy pilgrims who would spend time in retreat and leave a handsome remuneration at the end of their stay. Due to the tremendous wealth the abbey was able to amass, it became a venue not just for the pious but also the royal family and members of the nobility.

Most of the abbey that is visible today dates from the time of Hugh III. It was he who granted the Abbots the privilege of

Village of Bitter Lemons

From the car park, returning to the hub of activity, there is, in the village square, a choice of two trees that both lay claim to being 'The Tree of Idleness' written about by Lawrence Durrell in *Bitter Lemons*, his book about life on Cyprus. Opinion is sharply divided as to which is the real one.

On the one side are those in favour of the tree that is situated on the pavement outside the eponymous café and on the other are those in favour of the tree next to the coffee house which is adjacent to the ticket office for the Abbey. The former is a Japanese pagoda tree, the latter an ancient mulberry. It is usually the mulberry that comes out on top in an argument for it is under the shade of its old spreading branches that the men of the village sit on their rustic chairs, idling away the days, whilst playing a seemingly never-ending game of backgammon. The bucolic scene gives an air of romantic enchantment to the notion of indolence being manifested upon those unwary enough to sit in its shadow.

Regrettably Durrell never stated the type of tree when chronicling village life and he is no longer around to settle the argument. Whichever tree it is does not really matter as the story brings good trade to the village and is a constant source of debate.

Durrell's house, the buying and conversion of which is the subject matter of *Bitter Lemons* is very much evident as long as the visitor wants to climb the steep, almost perpendicular village street to get to it. It is not suitable for vehicular access as will be seen by those who make the pilgrimage.

It is an obvious conversion of a basic village cottage and even since Durrell's time has been added to. A simple glazed pottery plaque stating the house name above the front door is the only clue and easily missed.

The track at the rear of the house makes a pleasant return route passing old tumble-down cottages and the signs of one-time cottage industries like long abandoned and decaying olive presses. In some ways it makes a sombre picture but the visitor should not be too depressed by it because the villagers themselves are on the whole happy and cheerful and delight in the tourists their village attracts.

(cont'd overleaf)

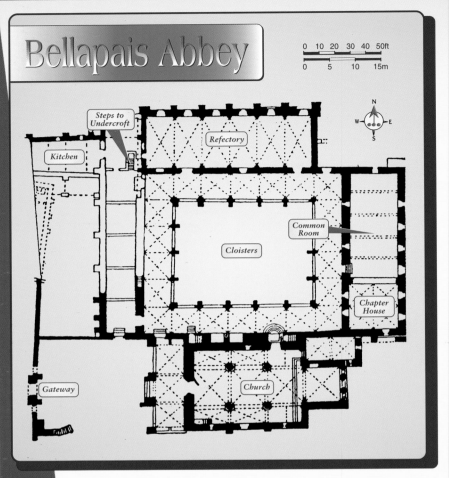

Bellapais Abbey

0 10 20 30 40 50ft
0   5   10   15m

Steps to
Undercroft

Kitchen

Refectory

N
W · E
S

Common
Room

Cloisters

Chapter
House

Gateway

Church

wearing a sword and golden spurs. Under the patronage of
Hugh IV, who was a devout catholic and promoter of the arts,
the abbey continued to develop. Hugh himself is recorded as
having a tremendous affection for Bellapais and spent a lot
of his time there building and improving on the monastic
quarters. The construction work is thought to have been
completed during the reign of Peter I and there was no
further building work thereafter.

When the Genoese overran the island in 1373/74 the
abbey of Bellapais became one of the victims of the
onslaught. The treasury was smashed open and all the
abbey wealth looted, including the piece of the true cross.

From this time on the abbey went into a decline and
never regained prominence. The monks of the order
degenerated into promiscuity and licentiousness, taking
wives and mistresses and only allowing their own sons

into the order as novices. They allowed the abbey building to fall into decay and lived a life far divorced from the rule of poverty, chastity and obedience.

When the Ottoman forces took the island they sacked the abbey and left it derelict. Whatever happened to the monks and their families is unknown, probably they dispersed into the surrounding villages and maybe their descendants are now part of the local community.

The abbey church was granted to the Orthodox faith and it continued to be used for worship until 1974. The rest of the monastic buildings crumbled and much of the stone was used by the villagers for the building of nearby cottages. Those buildings that remained roofed were used for farm implements and fodder stores and sheep grazed in the cloisters.

(cont'd overleaf)

Under British administration the building was put to little better use, being used by the army, and it continued to suffer the assaults of man. Gradually, since independence up to the present day the abbey buildings have undergone a steady programme of repair and are now one of the most popular and visited sites.

A walk around the abbey

The Abbey is undoubtedly a beautiful, elegant and impressive building, depicting a harmonious blending of Gothic styles throughout the stages of its development. The main buildings of the abbey form a square and the church has in front of it a small courtyard. This is defended by a machicolated **gatehouse** with drawbridge and occupies the south side of the buildings. The main entrance, storerooms and lodgings for the lay brothers in the western section and the kitchen in the north-west corner have all disappeared, the stone used elsewhere.

The refectory

Running parallel to the church along the entire northern section is the great refectory with six vaulted bays, lit at the eastern end by a small rose window. There are bay windows looking out to sea across the village of Ozanköy and the olive groves below. Also in the north wall there is a wall pulpit accessed by a stone staircase, for scripture readings at meal times. Beneath each window there is a drain through which the debris from the tables after meals would be swept away.

On the southern side of this very imposing room, which measures approximately 98ft (30m) long, 33ft (10m) wide and 36ft (11m) high, there is a row of high windows which look out over the roof of the cloisters. Two doors open onto the cloisters and above the door at the north end are the carved coat of arms of the Lusignan monarchs as Kings of Jerusalem, Kings of Cyprus and the quarters of Jerusalem and Cyprus together.

The two marble sarcophagi, most probably recycled from Salamis, were used by the monks as a lavabo. Situated as they are at the doorway to the refectory the monks would have washed their hands before meals. The upper sarcophagus was fitted with bungs or spigots, the holes for which can still be seen, and the lower one has a drain hole for the waste water.

& ABBEY •

The cloisters

The cloisters were built after the main church was completed sometime towards the end of the thirteenth century and well into the fourteenth century, and a slow walk around the three sides that are left is advised. The brackets at the base of the corbels are all different and there are some fascinating figures both human and animal, also some very elegant foliar carvings.

Leading off the south walk of the cloisters is the **night stair** by which the monks could reach the church for their night-time devotions, without disturbing the other inhabitants of the abbey. These stairs lead to the cloister roof, monks **dorter** (dormitory) and the treasury. There is nothing left of the dorter except the windows in the wall overlooking the cloister beside which is a small embrasure for the monks' personal possessions. These would have been few, as all worldly goods would have been given up, and probably consisted of only a prayer book, crucifix and rosary.

There is little to be seen in the **treasury** apart from the three safes built into the walls and evidence of the large hinges that held the doors.

Two other staircases can be used to descend to the cloisters; one passes beneath the treasury room and the other from the south-west corner of the cloister roof.

All three stairways have well worn steps and great care should be taken when descending.

Common room and chapter house

From the eastern cloister walk, two doors lead off, one into the common room or warming room and the other into the chapter house. It was above these that the dorter was situated and both rooms are now roofless.

The **chapter house** was the main administration office for the abbot and it was from here that he would issue the orders of the day. It is a square room with seating round the sides and richly carved brackets which at one time supported the ribs for the roof. There was a central column, long since disappeared, and in its place is an anachronism put there in the early 1900s: a hybridisation of a marble column with mismatched capital, which merely detracts from the Gothic carvings round the walls.

The adjacent **common room**, or warming room would have been the only area with heating available to the monks. There is now no evidence of the fireplace but it is thought that it would have been against the wall between this room and the chapter house. The monks carrying out the delicate task of manuscript

(cont'd overleaf)

illumination would have used this room – they merited a warm office, Bellapais can be very cold in winter.

Undercroft or storehouse

The undercroft of the abbey is the massive storehouse situated beneath the refectory and running the length of the north wall. It is divided into two separate rooms upheld by a line of huge columns, each supporting eight ribs for the roof. Access was gained from the kitchen area down a flight of steps and the rooms were used to store the victuals for the abbey community. The temperature remains reasonably the same throughout the year enabling the monks to maintain their foodstuffs in good condition.

Recently the undercroft floor has been paved and the two rooms are now used for exhibitions.

The abbey church

Entrance to the abbey church is from the courtyard which leads off the village square. There is an impressive porch with three bays. The walls to either side of the doorway show the remains of plaster and frescoes executed by Italian artists no earlier than the fourteenth century, most probably during the fifteenth century. They represent prophets and scenes from the life of Christ. Unfortunately they are in a bad state of preservation and it can only be supposition as to the identity of the characters depicted.

The church is joined to the south walk of the cloisters and there is a door, no longer used, that opens onto the night stair. The church is roughly square, with a nave, two aisles and transepts. The central nave leads up steps to the choir and altar, the aisles lead into arcaded transepts; the north transept leads into the sacristy and the south one may, at one time, have had a small altar at the eastern end.

The church is supported by squat pillars, that become half columns at the transepts with thickly carved capitals. The addition of a women's gallery above the main doorway is the work of the Orthodox religion, as is the iconostasis which now partitions the choir and altar from the main body of the church.

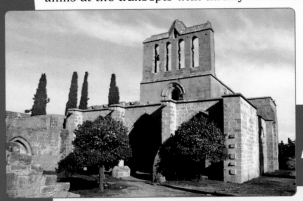

The church at Bellapais Abbey

The orthodox church of the Archangel Michael,
now the Girne Icon Museum

SITES OUTSIDE GIRNE

About 3 miles (5km) to the east of Girne, take the left turning for 'Tazkarts go-karting track' and the road leads down to the sea and **Hazreti Ömer Tekke** which is an important Islamic shrine. During the Arab raids in the seventh century, seven men from the Muawiya army were killed and buried in a cave. After the Ottoman conquest, the bodies were exhumed and reinterred. The shrine and a mosque were erected over the graves.

Neolithic Vrysi

After roughly 3 miles (5km) take the road for Acapulco/Esentepe and turn left into the Acapulco Holiday complex. On the rocky promontory above the restaurant is the Neolithic site of **Vrysi/Vrysin**.

This settlement dates to circa 4000BC and was inhabited for about 1,000 years. A preliminary investigation was made in 1969 and excavations began in 1972. It consists of houses, with only one room each, built partially underground, connected together by passages. This headland was selected owing to the depth of soil where the people could excavate hollows into which they built their stone houses. Floors were of plant fibres and wooden beams supported the roofs of reed thatch.

The finds include fragments of painted pottery, stone lamps, grinders, hammer stones, stone pillar figures and over 250 bone needles. It was the custom of these people to bury their dead beneath the floors of their houses.

Roman fish tanks

Heading west, take the turning on the right for Mare Monte Hotel. Where the road bears to the right for the hotel entrance, continue straight along the dirt track until a small farm is reached. Park your vehicle here and walk towards the shore. On the left, at the edge of the military area are rectangular shaped tanks cut into the rock, these are Roman fish tanks.

The Roman fishermen needed to keep their fish fresh so built the tanks to keep the fish alive before selling. They took advantage of the prevailing winds and tides to drive the sea water along the intake channels into the tanks. The easterly oriented channels provided exit passages for the stale, hot sea water. These channels can still be clearly seen. Behind the tanks, hewn from the rock are Roman tombs.

Ancient Lambousa

Due to the fact that an army enclosure is immediately to the west of the fish tanks, it is necessary to return to the main road, turn right and take the next right turning which is signposted 'Alsancak Beach'. This road follows a route down to the sea and there are red signs prohibiting entry to the land either side of the road. It is safe to proceed straight on.

The beach restaurant is situated at the site of the ancient harbour for the town of Lambousa. An important city kingdom of the early centuries BC, it was ruled by the Phoenicians during the fifth to fourth centuries BC. It became a thriving port during Roman and Byzantine times and then like so many of the coastal cities it was destroyed by the Arab raids of the seventh century AD.

Close the shore, west of the restaurant is the **monastery of Akhiropitos** containing the twin domed monastery church. Outside the monastic buildings is the church of St Eulambios and there is a curious building carved from a single block of limestone which is the chapel of St Eulambios. Excavations being carried out early in the twentieth century unearthed the 'Lambousa Treasure'. This consisted of some silver plates bearing very early hallmarks dating from the sixth century and coins and priceless artefacts, which are now displayed partly in the British Museum and in the Cyprus Museum in South Nicosia. Because this area is in military hands it is not open to visitors and photography is not permitted.

BEACHES IN THE GIRNE AREA

West coast beaches

This area covers the beaches primarily favoured by tourists, due to ease of access and the facilities on offer. Most are managed by either a hotel or restaurant, and are known under the same name. In return for keeping the beach clean a small entrance fee is charged. From Girne westwards the main road hugs the coast where the beaches are situated. Much of the tourist accommodation is to be found in this area.

Kervansaray Beach is a pretty, sandy cove just 4 miles (6.4km) from Girne. After driving through Karaoğlanoğlu turn right for Gülers Fish Bar. Park anywhere along the roadsides and walk down to the beach. A charge is made for the use of the sun loungers. There is a small beach bar serving drinks and ice cream, but no changing rooms. The restaurants overlooking the beach have a good selection of food.

It is quite magical here in the early evening, sipping a cool drink while watching the setting sun cast a golden glow over the gently lapping waves.

Next is **Sunset Beach** which is identified by the Peace and Freedom Monument dominating the sandy bay. This is a great place for children. A small island is only a short swim away from the shore; in fact it is almost possible to wade out to the island. Facilities are good but basic. The beach bar has a varied snack menu. There are showers and toilets, sun loungers and sunshades. Parking is no problem.

Around the headland is **Deniz Kızı (Mermaid) Beach**. A very attractive horseshoe bay. This beach belongs to two hotels, the Deniz Kızı and Deniz Kızı Royal, so it can be busy. Just above the beach is a large freshwater swimming pool. This is also open to the public. As well as the normal facilities some water sports are on offer. There are several steps down onto the sand so it is not suitable for people with walking difficulties.

Green Coast is a super area for snorkelling. The holiday village here has made a sandy beach; they have been successful to a certain extent, but where the sand finishes the stones begin. Beach shoes are a must. The restaurant is located at beach level and there are showers and toilets. The complex has a car park next to reception.

Alsancak Beach, a surprisingly attractive small sandy beach, has recently been open to the public. Look for the sign to Alsancak restaurant. After turning off the main road, head straight, ignoring the red army sign! The area was previously under military control and at the time of publication the warning has not yet been removed. A delightful local meal can be enjoyed while overlooking the sea.

Mare Monte is 5.6 miles (9km) from Girne. This long stretch of sand has plenty of sun loungers and sunshades. It is a popular beach with the locals so the weekends are normally busy. There are a great number of steps to the beach and when hot can feel like you are climbing a mountain!

The **LA Hotel** has a good sandy beach, which is well looked after. As well as the normal facilities you will also find water sports on offer.

East coast beaches

Along the east coast you will find beaches as nature intended; with very few facilities. Take the main road towards Gazimağusa and the Beşparmak Mountains. After travel-

ling roughly 6 miles (10km) the road forks. Take the left fork signposted **Esentepe** and **Acapulco Beach**.

Acapulco Beach is very easy to spot. A large square hotel has prominence here. Tickets for the beach are sold in the car park. This is a very well run sandy bay. There are plenty of sun loungers and sunshades. The beach bar here is particularly good, serving an excellent choice of snacks and meals, but prices can be high. Unlike the other beaches Acapulco has a nasty undercurrent when it is windy. Do take care.

Just a short distance further on is **Vakıflar Beach** or **Lara** as it is also called. This is a very interesting beach. On one side there are stones, to the other, sand. At the western side are huge slabs of smooth sandstone, which have created natural 'swimming pools' and rock pools. These are great to dive from. There is a small snack bar on the beach with toilets, changing rooms and showers. However there are very few sun loungers and hardly any shade.

The next beach is signposted **Turtle Beach** for it is here and at the next beach where the green and loggerhead turtles come and lay their eggs in the summer. Turtle beach is a long stretch of sand. To enjoy a day here it is preferable to take a picnic, sun shade and something to sit on. This goes for the rest of the beaches along this picturesque east coast. During the egg-laying season the beach area for sitting on is marked out with red painted stakes.

• KARAMAN VILLAGE •

At Karaoğlanoğlu there is a turning inland (signposted Edremit and Karaman), to the pretty mountain village of Karaman (Karmi). The road winds with some bad bends and sheer drops, but you will be rewarded with fantastic views. The picturesque houses give the impression that they are clinging on to the steep mountain slope.

After 1974, when the Greek Cypriot villagers moved south, these houses were left abandoned and started to fall into disrepair. The government came up with a policy for leasing the properties at a nominal fee to people willing to restore them. It is often referred to as the 'English' village although there are 'ex-pats' from most European countries residing there.

(cont'd overleaf)

Karaman church

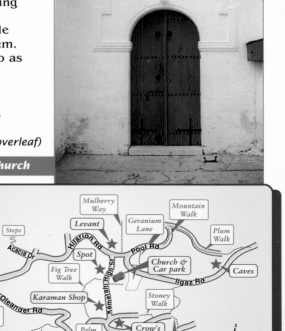

Karaman Village

Mulberry Way
Levant
Geranium Lane
Mountain Walk
Plum Walk
Steps
Acacia Dr
Hilarion Rd
Spot
Pool Rd
Church & Car park
Caves
Ilgaz Rd
Fig Tree Walk
Kemalatif High St
Karaman Shop
Stoney Walk
Hilarion Rd
Oleander Rd
Olive Walk
Treasure
Palm Walk
Crow's Nest
Ravine Walk
Cytrus Rd
Poppy Steps

KARAMAN VILLAGE

(cont'd from previous page)

There are indeed many similarities to a small rural village in England. The roads have names such as 'Figtree Walk', 'The High Street', and 'Acacia Drive' with houses called 'Cobblers' and 'Dingley Dell'. An English couple runs the 'Crows Nest' pub where the standard fare is pie and chips, and there is even a small 'corner shop'. This delightful mountain village becomes home for many tourists throughout the summer, however the winters are bleak. It becomes very damp and loses the sunlight early in the day, in fact for one month of winter it gets no sun at all.

Parking can be found next to the church, which is open every Sunday from 10am-1pm. An interesting talk is given by the self-appointed curator at 12.00pm, who has lived here for over twenty years. Although the icons are all nineteenth century, the church is worth a visit.

Bronze Age cemetery

Before reaching Karaman a track branches off to the left, to the Bronze Age cemetery which is signposted with a yellow sign. This site dates from the Middle Bronze Age, and is therefore older than the Royal Tombs at Salamis. There are a number of burial chambers grouped around the *dromos* (approach).

In the tomb numbered six a carved female figure was found whose prominent reproductive organs suggest that she is a fertility goddess. This is the earliest relief of a human figure found in Cyprus to date. In another grave some blue beads thought to have come from Egypt and a Minoan *kamares* (cup) were found. These represent the first evidence of trading links with Egypt and Crete.

Village walks

There are many beautiful walks in this area with easy access to the mountain tracks. Karaman was the last place on the island receiving its post by donkey, this service finished in 1959. Post is now delivered to the village post office and residents collect it from there.

Such a pretty village deserves to be explored. By using the map on the previous page, follow these simple village walks.

Walk 1

Head north along the High Street in the direction of the Crow's Nest pub. At the pub turn right down the steep hill. Turn left from the car park into Citrus Road.

Turn left up Poppy Steps and at the top turn right. When the track meets İlgaz Road turn left and this will bring you back to the church car park.

Walk 2

From the T-junction at Levant Restaurant bear west along Almond Way. Continue by joining Pool Road. At the T-junction turn right onto Mountain Walk. Mountain Walk becomes Plum Walk, and there are some superb views along this route.

At the end of Plum Walk descend down to İlgaz Road. Turn right, past the caves back to the village.

Alternatively continue to the left, the road doubles back on itself and heads upwards between two houses. The route now begins to climb the lower slopes of the mountain. The sharp ascent meets the forestry road; although the climb is steep the views are breathtaking.

Either continue further up the Forestry Road or return back, taking the İlgaz Road.

Walk 3

Head north along the High Street. After passing the Spot Bar turn right down Fig Tree Walk. At the T-junction (behind the Crow's Nest) turn right.

Next T-junction turn right. Next T-junction right again. Pass Ravine Walk and join Oleander Road. T-junction turn right onto Hilarion Road and walk back to the village.

Alternatively follow Hilarion Road to The Treasure restaurant for refreshments and a wonderful view from the terrace.

Walk 4

At the eastern end of the High Street take Hilarion Road. Follow the road to Acacia Drive. About 110 yards (100m) along Acacia Drive you will see steps climbing upwards. 252 steps later you will have a wonderful view of the village, the mountains and the coastline.

2

The Mountain
Castles

St Hilarion Castle, high above Girne, showing the three distinct levels of accommodation

The three castles built along the Beşparmak mountain range are similar and yet retain their own distinct characteristics. Whether you are looking for suberb views, a sense of what it was like to live in those times, or a day out, read the following descriptions to choose which appeals most. All route directions are given from Girne.

Brief summary

Each of the castles started out as a Byzantine fort and lookout post. Once the French Lusignan dynasty came to power and pursued their Crusades against what they perceived as the bloody infidel, they strengthened and enlarged the original forts and turned them into imposing fortresses to deter any invader.

St Hilarion Castle

To the west just above Girne stands the castle of St Hilarion; named after a hermit who once inhabited the summit. Its highest point is a little under 2,400ft (732m) and because so much of the royal apartments and barracks remain it is probably the most impressive. St Hilarion is built on three levels, each of which was guarded by a gatehouse and entirely self-contained.

The lower level consisted of stables, an armoury and barracks.

The middle level contains some impressive knights' quarters, the Great Hall (sadly burnt out during the June 1995 fire and not repaired at time of writing) and the shell of a Byzantine chapel, with some just discernible fresco remains in vibrant colours.

The upper level consists of winding and very narrow steps up to Prince John's Tower and the royal apartments. The views over Girne and the surrounding villages are splendid and from the royal apartments truly breathtaking.

Buffavento Castle

Going eastwards, approximately 10 miles (16km) as the crow flies is Buffavento. Truly buffeted by the wind, it is the highest and most inaccessible of the castles; a 4.2 mile (6.8km) drive along a rough track is followed by a 45-minute walk up the mountain path. A stout pair of walking boots and a stick are strongly recommended to those keen and fit enough to attempt the climb.

At 3,100ft (945m) this castle has the most spectacular and panoramic views over the whole of the Mesaoria plain and miles of the northern coastline.

Largely ruined, all that exists are a few rooms, some with cisterns beneath them and roofless chambers open to the elements. One can but wonder at the impressive feat of architecture and expertise of the builders.

The castle is under the care of the military forces and has restricted opening hours. Please check the days of opening with a local guide.

Kantara Castle

Thirty miles (48km) further east at the gateway of the Karpas Peninsula is Kantara Castle. Easily the most accessible and, due to the extent of the almost complete buildings, the easiest in which to envisage life as it was in the late Middle Ages.

It stands at just over 2,000ft (610m) and is constructed around the entire circumference of the mountain peak on which it was built.

There are huge barrack rooms, a dungeon block (more correctly an 'oubliette', of which the French were inordinately fond). Magnificent and extensive storerooms and again cisterns for collecting water.

On a clear day the view along the fertile north coast, up the length of the Karpas Peninsula and down southwards across Salamis Bay to Gazimağusa is quite astounding.

· CASTLE OF ST HILARION ·

The westernmost of the three mountain castles, St Hilarion looks down over the town of Girne and maintains a commanding view east along the range of mountains to distant Kantara.

History of St Hilarion

The mountain lookouts were built early in the seventh century to give advance warning of Arab raiders. During Byzantine rule they were enhanced into well-defended forts.

The French added apartments for the knights, the construction of cisterns to collect water, and chapels for worship.

The castle pre-dates Richard the Lionheart's take-over of the island. The Byzantine church in the middle ward has traces of tenth century frescoes and there was possibly a monastic order housed here. In 1228 when Frederick II was attempting to overthrow the kings of Cyprus, the regent at that time, John of Ibelin, made the castle

The legend of the hermit

There is no adequately documented evidence for calling the castle St Hilarion though it is known that there was a hermit of that name who dwelt upon the summit. According to legend he was extremely deaf and was totally impervious to the shrieks of the demons who had been the only inhabitants of the mountain peak before him. Disgusted at their inability to make him go, they departed, leaving the mountain in peace.

It is known that the Byzantine fort was called Didymos, meaning twin, from the twin peaks that form the top of the castle defences. The French corrupted this to *Dieu d'Amour*, maybe confusing a mixture of legends and believing that this was the castle of Venus/Aphrodite who during her period on Earth had been Queen of Cyprus.

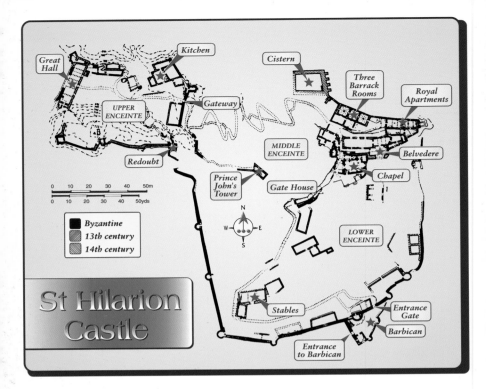

St Hilarion
Castle

Map labels:
Great Hall · Kitchen · Cistern · Three Barrack Rooms · Royal Apartments · UPPER ENCEINTE · Gateway · Belvedere · MIDDLE ENCEINTE · Chapel · Redoubt · Prince John's Tower · Gate House · LOWER ENCEINTE · Stables · Entrance Gate · Barbican · Entrance to Barbican

N W E S

Byzantine
13th century
14th century

0 10 20 30 40 50m
0 10 20 30 40 50yds

available as a refuge to the wives of the Cypriot nobility. As the island stayed under a state of semi-siege the castle played a prominent role in the island's defences and after the victory of John of Ibelin at the battle of Agridi (Ağirdağ) in June 1232 the island was liberated and returned to a state of peace and quiet.

For the next 150 years St Hilarion was used as a summer palace and the knights would practice their martial skills on the jousting grounds, while their ladies had a grandstand view from the belvedere in the middle ward.

After the Genoese rampage of 1373/74 Prince John of Antioch took refuge in the castle and it was from the tower now known as Prince John's tower that the gullible John threw one by one, members of his faithful Bulgarian guard. He had been persuaded by his evil, scheming sister-in-law, Eleanor the Queen Mother, to believe that his bodyguards were planning to murder him. He took terrible revenge without first finding out the truth. One of the guards escaped with his life and fled the castle. Shortly after John too left the imposing height of his tower and departed St Hilarion, never to return.

When the Venetians took over the island in 1489 they dismantled the castle deeming it worthless in warfare as it would not have withstood the power of cannon. They concentrated their efforts on strengthening the major cities, and left the castle to crumble, unwanted and uninhabited, except maybe by those spirits that still dwelt among the twin peaks.

The Byzantine church, set in the middle enceinte of St Hilarion

Getting there

To get to the castle from Girne take the main road out of town heading south, signposted Lefkoşa (Nicosia). The dual carriageway leading off the roundabout on the ring road climbs the mountain range, passing the black silhouette of Atatürk perched high on the hillside on the right. At the top of this climb, about 50 yards (45m) before the mountain pass there is a turning to the right signposted St Hilarion Castle. Take this turning and follow the route as directed by the army signs. It is a controlled road and stopping and taking photographs is forbidden.

The road is narrow in places and careful driving is essential on the hairpin bends. A Turkish army Commando camp is on the right and the route continues to ascend. Views of Girne appear to the right and the road reaches its highest point with a clear vista towards the twin peaks of Didymos ahead. You may not stop at this point which has a war memorial to the left. The road descends slightly, passing the **old jousting grounds**, now used by the army as a rifle range. At the end of the range the road becomes derestricted and there is a pull-in space. Photographs of the castle may be taken at this point. However, it is advisable not to stop if the army are actually on the range. The road continues to the base of the castle walls and there is ample parking.

Tour of the castle

The castle is built in three separate parts, each is self-contained and would have been inhabited by its own community of servants, knights and nobles, and royalty.

Lower ward

The entrance gate to the **bailey** or lower ward is guarded by a small **barbican**. The main entrance has a machicoulis over it with some fine carvings. The outer bailey wall has battlements linked by six semi-circular towers and a walkway for the sentries between each tower.

The lower ward contained such offices as an armoury, stores and stabling. After entering the main gate the path climbs to the left and follows a course along the line of the southernmost battlements. Underground on the left is a large cistern and as the pathway turns to the right there is another cistern and a **stable block**.

Middle ward

Climbing onwards the archway to the second ward is entered. On the right are two flights of stone steps, the first leads up to the floor above the entrance gate and provides a wonderful vantage point over the lower ward. The second leads to the **Byzantine chapel**. The pillars of this chapel have undergone restoration. It has been tastefully done and the remains of frescoes are dimly discernible on the walls.

On the outer wall at the western end, the French additional masonry has been broken away and through the gaps it is quite possible to see the vibrant colours of some late Byzantine wall paintings. The chapel was adopted by the French for Catholic worship and it has several small rooms leading off it: sacristy, confessional and private chapel.

Wandering through the dozens of still extant rooms of the middle ward takes time and should not be missed. It is well worth taking the steps that lead from the chapel down to a dark tunnel which overlooks the burnt out shell of the great hall.

Before June 1995 and the great fire that engulfed so much of the mountainside, this was used for serving refreshments. There was a balcony with views over the north coast and Girne. Sadly, only the charred debris remains and it will be many years before such expensive and extensive restoration can take place.

At the eastern end of the passage is the **belvedere**. Here the ladies would sit and watch the knights on the jousting ground below. Doorways lead off into small chambers, and flights of steps lead round the walls of the apartments, now largely roofless. There are a couple of **latrine rooms** on this route and then a flight of steel steps leading up to a viewing point which is almost at the top of a four-storey building. The view east along the mountain range is spectacular.

Descending the flight of metal stairs the approach is to some storerooms and barracks on the right. There are now more steps to ascend and the path continues upward to the very top passing on the right an enormous **water cistern** built partly into the face of the mountain and on the eastern side supported by massive buttresses.

Visitors with children must take care as there are long drops everywhere.

Upper ward

The ascent to the upper ward is long and winding. Just before reaching the entrance gate to the topmost section of the castle, there is a junction. To the left a flight of steps leads to **Prince John's tower**, worth visiting just to contemplate the fate of the hapless Bulgarian guard.

The main entranceway is guarded by a strong gate and on entering, the **kitchen apartments** are to the right. Steps to the left lead to a high **lookout tower** and from this point it is possible to look south over the mountain towards Lefkoşa.

Returning to level ground the path passes a fenced-in cistern full of murky water on the right and leads into the only relatively intact buildings that comprised the royal apartments on this level. There are the remains of the **Great Hall**, the western wall fallen away down the mountain and above, the boudoir of the plotting Queen Eleanor. No doubt she gazed out at the wonderful view while devising her next malicious scheme.

The views are truly breathtaking; if by this time the climber has any breath left, it is uplifting to just sit and gaze out over the countryside towards the mountain village of Karaman. Far below, the coastline drifts sinuously away towards the west and as far as the eye can see there is uncluttered beauty.

The descent to the car park is only slightly less tricky but will take much less time and the intrepid climber can at least reward himself with a cold drink at the little café by the car park.

Strong shoes, a walking stick, camera, binoculars and a bottle of water are recommended accessories for scaling St Hilarion.

• BUFFAVENTO CASTLE •

Getting there

The only route to Buffavento is from the main road that leads from Girne over the mountains via the Beşparmak mountain pass. As the road reaches its highest point and before descending the southern slopes there is a turning to the right. There is also a yellow and black sign which has been defaced with spray paint pointing the way to the castle.

The road is accessible by car but the first 800 yards (730m) is rough and needs to be driven with care. It is a 4.2 mile (6.8km) drive along a road which is evidently a military access route. There are red signs forbidding entrance strategically placed along the track. The signs mean that there must be no deviation from the route and it must be followed strictly.

Buffavento, because it is in the hands of the military, has restricted opening hours and these are regularly subject to change. Check with a local guide for the opening times. It is not unknown for the military to post a sentry on the access road who will advise the visitor that the castle is closed even on days when it should be open. Entry to the castle is free.

The car parking area is a clearing on the hillside with a solitary olive tree and the memorial to the

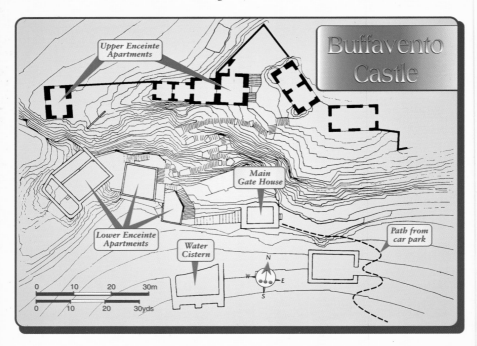

Beşparmak mountain ridge near Buffavento

crew of a Turkish Airlines aircraft who perished in a crash in 1988.

Glancing upwards to the mountain top, Buffavento is plainly discernible among the rocky peaks. At first glimpse it would seem that the climb to reach the top requires the skill of a mountaineer. However there is a gravelled pathway that winds on a fairly gentle ascent up the slopes. It takes approximately three quarters of an hour to make the trip, with the occasional stop to admire the view and in spring to seek out the wild flowers that pattern the hillside.

History of Buffavento

It is known that there was a fortress of some type here before Richard I took the island from Isaac Comnenus. The first definite information comes from 1232 when the wife of Balian of Ibelin took refuge in Buffavento while her husband was campaigning against the attempted usurpation of the island by Fredrick II.

Due to the inaccessible position and tremendous height, minimising the chances of escape, the castle was used as a prison to hold those found guilty of particular crimes against the state. These included the naïve John Visconti who had tried to warn his friend King Peter I of the Queen's infidelities, only to find himself disbelieved and found guilty of slander. After being tortured and imprisoned in Girne he was transferred to Buffavento and starved to death.

Buffavento was also used as a lookout for passing ships that might pose a threat to the island. Flares ignited on the top sent instant messages of danger to Lefkoşa, Girne, St Hilarion and Kantara. Buffavento is a commanding observation post and a safe place of refuge. At 3,100ft (945m) it is the highest and most cleverly constructed of the three mountain castles.

Tour of the castle

The buildings of the castle form two distinct groups and entry to the lower group is made through the **gatehouse**, passing on the way the ruins of what may have been a **barbican**. On the left, further on and below the level of the main buildings can be seen the remains of a large **cistern**.

Most of the buildings of this section are in poor repair with the exception of the gatehouse and the next building reached up a flight of stone steps. Both these rooms are roofed and would give adequate shelter in bad weather and provide shade in summer. The latter has an underfloor cistern. The other buildings at this level consist of little more than the remains of walls and afford wonderful views over the plain.

To reach the upper level of the castle it is another 70ft (21m) climb up to the roofless buildings of the highest point. It is from here that the view is a panoramic 360° and on a clear day Gazimağusa, Lefkoşa, the length of the panhandle and the Turkish mainland are clearly visible. It is very easy to understand how the castle acquired its name, for truly it is buffeted by the winds.

A bold, daring feat of military engineering using mostly the limestone rock from the escarpment on which it is built, Buffavento has no defensive structures as have St Hilarion and Kantara. This is obviously because at such a height and in such an impregnable position, with sheer drops on every side, the addition of battlements was unnecessary.

As at St Hilarion, the Venetians dismantled parts of Buffavento, rendering it useless and destroying the stairway that led from the lower to the upper level. The stone steps have only been reinstated during the twentieth century, making the final ascent slightly easier.

Buffavento is a castle only of interest to those with a fascination for military architecture. It is an arduous climb even on a cool day and is certainly not recommended in the hottest months of summer. Those indomitable enough to want to scale its heights should always be prepared with good walking shoes and a bottle of water.

• KANTARA CASTLE •

For castle lovers, Kantara is the most complete and the most romantic of the three mountain fortresses. It is also, according to legend, the castle of one hundred and one rooms. Whoever is lucky enough to find the one hundred and first is sure to enter paradise. There are guide books that state St Hilarion is the castle of one hundred and one rooms. One can only think their research suspect as this is totally erroneous.

A scenic journey

From Girne, Kantara is the most distant castle to reach and a whole day should be given over to the expedition. If this trip is taken to encompass all there is to see it will take approximately six hours at a fairly leisurely pace. By far the most scenic route is the coast road running eastwards. It is approximately 45 miles (72.4km) from Girne to Kantara and every mile of the journey has something of interest.

Follow the main Gazimağusa road out of Girne and then take the turning left, signposted **Esentepe**, **Tatlisu**, **'Acapulco'** and **'Alagadi Green Turtles Beach'**. Follow the coastline and enjoy the calm of the quiet roads. Other traffic is rare and usually consists of one to two other tourist cars, the local bus and tractors. The latter outnumber any other form of transport, as this is predominantly an agricultural area. It is along this fertile coastline that a large majority of the fruit and vegetables are grown. Vast polythene tunnels will be seen growing a rich harvest of tomatoes, cucumbers, green beans, aubergines etc. Fields full of watermelons and the small sweet honeydew melons, grown during the summer months, are brought into the local towns and villages by the truckload and cost the equivalent of only pennies per kilogram.

There will also be large flocks of sheep and goats. Stop the car and listen to the mellifluous sound of the goat bells. The shepherds will always wave a greeting and the pastoral scene makes for a wonderful photographic opportunity. In some places the convolutions of the road mean driving has to be taken slowly

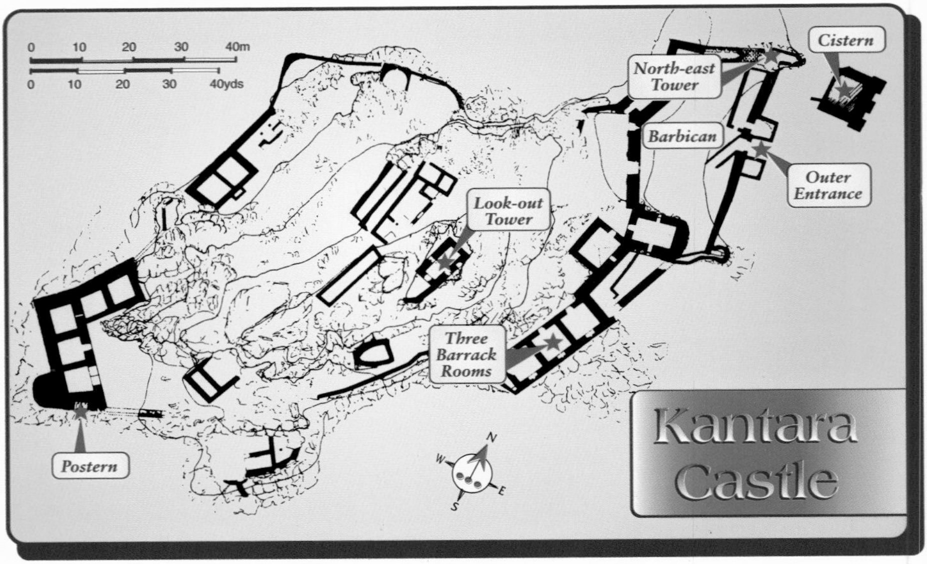
0 10 20 30 40m
0 10 20 30 40yds
Cistern
North-east Tower
Barbican
Outer Entrance
Look-out Tower
Three Barrack Rooms
Postern
N
W
E
S
Kantara Castle

Kantara Castle, the north-east tower on the left, and the Karpas peninsula stretching into the distance

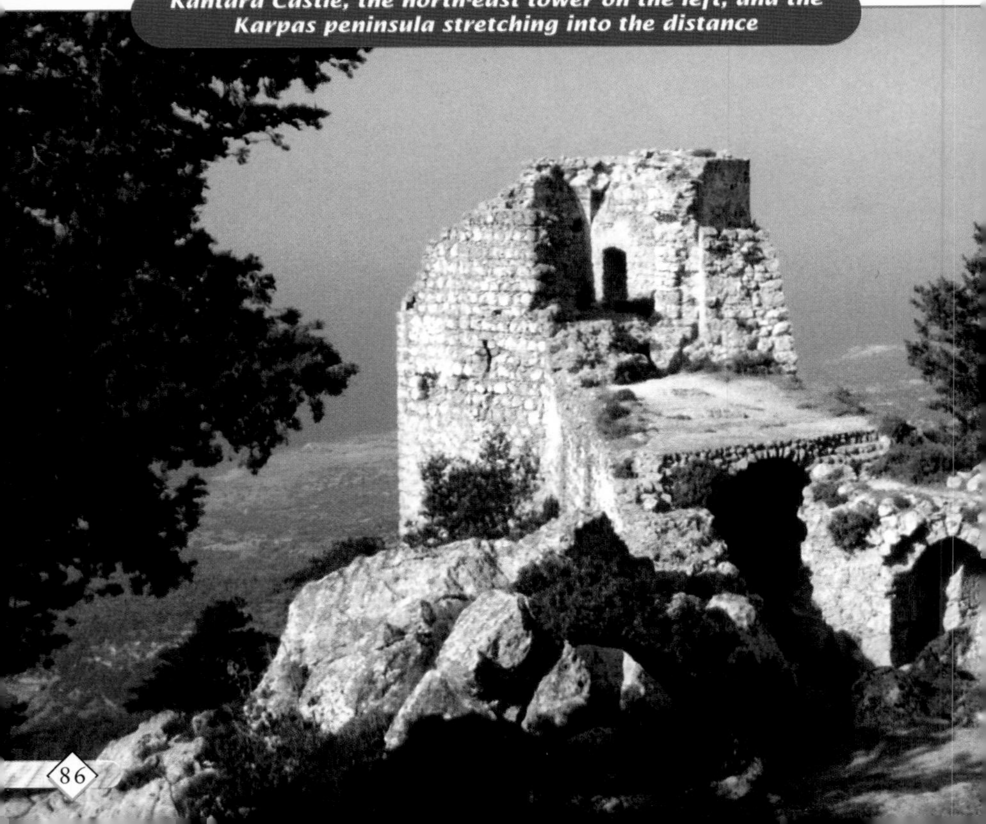

and it is because this is such a circuitous route that the trip takes so long. However it is well worth it, for along this coastline there are frequent reminders of Cyprus' history.

Historic remnants

Long abandoned and roofless carob warehouses remind the traveller of the once great wealth of carob export. The storehouses are not now used for their original purpose and instead provide a pound for sheep and cattle at night and are also utilised as boat sheds.

All along this coastline is the evidence of hoped for tourism. Greek-built hotels and restaurants, half finished, long abandoned and neglected, bear silent witness to the building congestion that would have taken place had not the island been divided in 1974.

There are stretches of wild rocky coast interspersed with short sandy patches. This part of the coastline is largely untended and it is impossible to escape the debris that is washed ashore. Unfortunately many of the countries surrounding the Mediterranean have no domestic refuse disposal policy other than to dump it in the sea. Consequently anything that floats is washed up on the beaches. Driving along the cliffs of soft limestone, there are frequent carvings in the rock, created by the wind and rain, resulting in an almost surreal landscape and contributing to the feeling of solitude.

Do not take the turning to Mersinlik, which is also signposted 'Kantara'. Continue along the coast for about 4 miles (6.4km) and **Kaplıca Restaurant** and beach will be on your left. The beach is a clean sandy horseshoe bay. Kept clean of rubbish, it is a superb place to swim. The restaurant serves good local fish with salad and chips.

Nestling in the foothills of the mountains is **Kaplıca** village and, high above, the imposing presence of Kantara castle. The route from the restaurant is quite straightforward. Take the next turning on the right and enter the village through an avenue of ancient pine trees. Climb steadily upwards, the road is narrow but has a good tarmac surface and the occasional passing place.

On reaching Kantara village follow the signs to the castle, which is about another 3 miles (5km) distant. Parking is right under the base of the castle and there is a lethargic ticket seller in attendance.

The majesty of Kantara is obvious from first sight. Fortunately it is the most complete of the castles. Many of the barracks, storerooms and towers would only need a sweep out and a coat of whitewash to make them quite habitable. It is easy to envisage life here as it would have been in the late Middle ages.

History of Kantara

Kantara appears in documented history at the same time as Hilarion and Kyrenia castles. In 1228 it was occupied by the troops of the Emperor Frederick II while he was attempting his take-over of the island. The Imperialists were beaten in 1229 to retake the castle again in 1232 before being finally trounced.

When the Genoese overran the island and occupied Gazimağusa, they failed to storm the castle. James I added to the fortifications and from this vantage point his garrison was able to keep watch over Gazimağusa and the surrounding area. Many of the buildings date from this period.

After the Venetian take-over, the castle was deemed of no further use and partially dismantled. Perched on a rocky summit at the eastern end of the mountain range, Kantara at just over 2,000ft (610m) is the lowest of the three mountain castles. Even so it has a commanding view up the Karpas Peninsula, all along the northern coastline and far down across the plain to the city of Gazimağusa. From this position it was able to exchange flare signals with Buffavento and St Hilarion to the west.

Layout of the castle

A short climb up a gravelled path leads to the outer entrance to the **barbican**. Slightly lower and to the right of this entrance is a vast **water cistern**. The channels leading into this water tank are plainly visible as one climbs the pathway from the barbican to the entrance of the main enceinte.

The castle is built around the entire perimeter of the mountain peak. In places there is just the crumbling curtain wall to prevent a fall to certain death. At other points around the boundary there are barracks, latrines, more cisterns and lookout towers. The buildings are scattered among the rocks, which must have made negotiating a route round the castle, particularly at night, especially hazardous. Only the lower floors of the complex assortment of buildings remain. The upper floors have long since been thrown down the mountain.

Tour of the castle

The best route round the castle begins after entering the **gateway** to the enceinte. Keep to the left and immediately at the top of the rise there are rectangular chambers. In the first there is a grating which covers the entrance to an underground room that was used as a **prison**.

Keeping close to the walls, climb the rocky path and turn left, clamber down a few steps to pass **three barrack rooms**. There is a latrine at the far end. Painted arrows on the walls give some guidance along this route but there is a perilous drop to the left and a water cistern on the right.

Keeping to the path along the cliff edge the next set of buildings are at the western end. The first may have been a chapel or just a storehouse as are the other rooms in this block. There is also an underground cistern, very much open and unguarded. The curtain wall now follows the line of the rock face and the remains of another building are hidden among foliage. There is a wonderful view of Kaplıca village and the two sandy bays below.

On attaining the central plateau of the castle, the **lookout tower** and highest point is a climb over easily scaled rocks to the right. There is little remaining here except one rather ornate window, which may possibly have formed part of the royal apartments.

By far the most impressive of the buildings is the **north-east tower**. Entry is on the left of the main entrance looking eastwards. There is a long passageway with arrow slits looking north-west and then a square corner chamber. Off this leads the narrow part of the tower in which the archers would stand armed with their long bows. From here they could not be seen but with deadly accuracy a fine bowman could dispatch many an enemy below.

There is no doubt that the views from Kantara are as spectacular as from any other vantage point and this castle is particularly beautiful in springtime. There is an abundance of wild flowers to be seen and the area is very popular with botanists and walkers.

Return to Girne

An alternative route back to Girne is to return to the village of Kantara and take the left turn marked **Turnalar** and **Boğaztepe**. This leads down to the main Karpas to Gazimağusa road. When reaching this road turn right for Gazimağusa and continue until the turning for Salamis is on the left. 300 yards (274m) further on the right is the turning for Lefkoşa. Take this road and drive on to the village of **Mutluyaka**, joining the main Gazimağusa and Lefkoşa road and then follow the signs for Girne.

• MOUNTAIN DRIVING

There are many varied routes to take through the mountain range. To make sure you have an enjoyable day please take note of the following:

1. It is not advisable to go after rain as the tracks become dangerous when wet.

2. The majority of tracks are best negotiated with a jeep. Not necessarily because the 4WD is needed, but the suspension is too low on saloon cars.

3. Take your own refreshments, there are many picnic sites to enjoy.

4. Check the water and oil on the vehicle and start the journey with a full tank of fuel.

5. If you get out of the vehicle to admire the flora and fauna, be sure to stay on the paths. Snakebites are extremely rare but not unheard of.

6. Do not forget your camera!

7. All distances are approximate.

8. Many of the paths and tracks that lead off from the main routes are forestry paths. Normally they are not signposted and in terrible condition.

ROUTES •

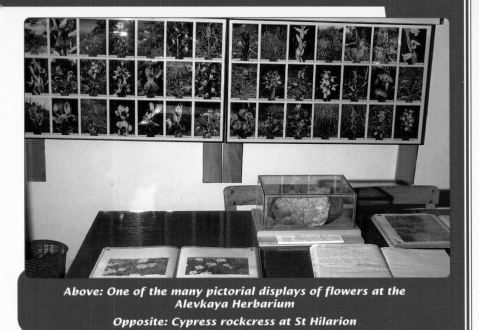

Above: One of the many pictorial displays of flowers at the Alevkaya Herbarium

Opposite: Cypress rockcress at St Hilarion

Herbarium Route

Round trip approximately 3 hours • 46 miles (74km)

The track is rough, but with care it is possible to drive this route with a Renault 9

Take the main road out of Girne heading east towards Gazimağusa. Follow the road for approximately 5 miles (8km) and as you pass the sign for **Acapulco/Esentepe** the road starts to climb through the Beşparmak (Five Fingers) mountains.

Tragically the great fire of June 1995 destroyed the pine forests on either side of the road. It started on a Tuesday in June, and burnt for 35 miles (56km) along the mountains, taking all the pine forests with it. The fire lasted for 4 days and in the end could only be put out by helicopters dropping water bombs. This area has since been cultivated with the planting of many saplings. The views of the coastline are stunning and on a clear day the Turkish mainland can be seen.

(cont'd overleaf)

• MOUNTAIN DRIVING

After roughly 3 miles (5km) the power station comes into view. Easily identified by the red and white striped chimney. Within a mile the road reaches the top of the pass and on the left is the Beşparmak Café. Turn left here. There is a small sign for the Herbarium and a new large sign warning of the danger of fire. It states that the lighting of a fire of any description is illegal and the penalty is a large fine or imprisonment.

The views as you drive along are fantastic and you should take a leisurely pace. After a mile, look across the valley, which is a picture of vibrant colours in the springtime, full of wild anemones.

Sourp Magar Monastery

After driving for about 4 miles (6.5km) slow down and start to look down into the valley. There are the remains of the Sourp Magar Monastery. Originally the monastery belonged to a small Coptic Christian community who dedicated it to St Magar. The access road is another mile ahead on the left. The large picnic area here is wonderfully shaded and a popular spot for the locals, who love to eat, drink and make merry. At the time of writing this road was closed due to restoration, but you could proceed on foot.

In the fifteenth century the monastery passed to the Armenians and was a famous place of pilgrimage for Armenians on their way to the Holy Land prior to 1974.

The Herbarium

At the T-junction on the start of the metalled road, **Karaagaç** is signposted to the left and the **Northern Cyprus Herbarium** is to the right. Housed in the Alevkaya Forest Station, it was established by the resident English botanist Dr Deryck Viney in November 1989. There are nearly 1,250 pressed and preserved plants as well as photographic displays and sketches. The Herbarium is open between 8am-4pm every day.

Next to the Herbarium is an excellent **restaurant**, which serves delicious lamb chops and kebabs freshly cooked on the barbecue. This restaurant is normally full all day long on Sunday, come summer or winter.

This route follows the left turn to Karaagaç, passing one of the mountain reservoirs.

Antiphonitis Church

At the next fork, Esentepe is to the right and Karaagaç to the left. **Antiphonitis** is in this area. Drive past the turning for Karaagaç and follow the road through the beautiful forest. There is a sharp bend left for Esentepe, take the rough track east. Proceed with care and caution for roughly 3 miles (5km) until a cross-roads is reached with a short square column. Antiphonitis is on the left. Please leave your vehicle at the cross-roads and walk the last 100 yards (90m) down into the valley as you need a jeep to tackle this part of the track.

Antiphonitis ('Christ of the Echo') is a very pretty twelfth century church. The dome is supported by eight columns, four of them built into the walls and four detached. It is the last surviving example of this style in Cyprus. The western porch and arcade were added in the fifteenth century and are fine examples of Gothic architecture. It is thought that many of the frescoes have been destroyed or stolen but some admirable examples remain. The paintings in the sanctuary and in the south-west sector of the nave date from the late twelfth century. The Virgin Mary is depicted in the apse flanked by the Archangels Gabriel and Michael. The Baptism of Christ is well preserved on the column in the south-west corner. The other frescoes date from the fifteenth century. Antiphonitis is now kept locked. You must apply to the custodian of Kyrenia Castle who will arrange for a member of the Antiquities Department to open the church.

Return to the original route, turn left and approximately 2 miles (3km) along this road is a fresh water spring. This is a pretty area with date, carob and fir trees giving plenty of shade. Shortly after is a fork in the road, carry straight on. This is Karaağac village. Proceed at a slow pace, the bends are bad out of the village.

At the next junction, which is about 3 miles (5km) from Karaağac, take the left turning signposted Beşparmak, Girne and Lefkoşa. You have now joined the coast road.

'Tank' Route

Round trip approximately 3 hours • 37 miles (60km)
This track is rough and should only be driven in a jeep

Head west out of Girne on the main **Güzelyurt** road passing through Karaoğlanoğlu. Follow the road for approximately 8.3 miles (13.4km) and turn left for **Lapta**.

After the Arab raids during the seventh century, the inhabitants of Lambousa relocated to Lapta. Its perpetual

(cont'd overleaf)

Antiphonitis church, twelfth century fresco of the Archangel Michael

spring made the area a centre of agriculture. Pottery was manufactured in large quantities and exported. The **Başpinar springs** still provide water for the citrus groves. In the centre of the village turn right into **Azerbaycan Sokak** and follow the Başpinar signs. The road starts to climb.

Antiphonitis church hidden away in the wooded mountains near Esentepe

Turn left after 3 miles (5km) along a gravel track with 'No picnic' signs. Take the left-hand fork, and very shortly you will pass a round water tank, look to the right for a panoramic view. Within 2.5 miles (4km) is another water tank with an ancient wild fig, and just past a fork in the road, bear right.

The left track here leads to the village of **Ilgaz**, renowned for beautiful almond blossom in the spring. At the old forestry buildings turn right and continue until a T-junction is reached.

The huge transmission aerial belonging to the army is on the left and this is in a restricted military area. ASKERİ BÖLGE GİRİLMEZ means 'army zone, no entry' so you must proceed to the right.

After roughly a mile (2km) a crashed army tank has been cemented into the mountainside. This Turkish tank crashed on 2nd August 1974 and paints a very vivid picture of the past conflict. In another mile (2km) the view starts to open out across the Mesaoria plan and then bends back around for a different view northwards. The road starts to descend and there is another round water tank and a fresh water spring. A mile (2km) further on the track joins a metalled road with cross-roads. Turn right. This road leads into **Karsiyaka** village. Drive straight through the village and down to the main road turning right for Girne.

(cont'd overleaf)

'Flag' Route

Round trip approximately 1 hour • 22 miles (35km)

This track is rough and should only be driven in a jeep

Take the road to **Bellapais**. Before the village, there is a bad bend with a right turning to **Ambelia Holiday Village**. Head towards Ambelia. The road climbs sharply and there is another fork, this time stay left. Very shortly the tarmac road ends, stay right at this point and the road passes a small white Greek Church. The views here are splendid over the abbey and village.

After climbing for about 2 miles (3km) a level plateau is reached with the remains of an old lime kiln on the right. There is a mixture of barren and cultivated land here. At the bottom of the hill, there is a signpost for Beylerbeyi (Bellapais), pointing in the wrong direction! At the next small junction just past this sign, turn right. Within half a mile (1km) is another small junction keep left here, and follow the road downwards.

As you approach the village of **Taşkent** look up left and immediately above on the hillside is the world's largest painted flag. It is the flag of the Turkish Republic of Northern Cyprus and was painted in one night. The writing on the left is a quote by Kemal Atatürk and translates as 'Happy is the man who can say he is a Turk'.

Bear right. The views in front are of Lefkoşa. Take the sign for **Dikmen** and Girne on the right, Lefkoşa and Gazimağusa are to the left. The land here is agricultural with a quarry on the right. After 3 miles (5km) Dikmen village is reached. After passing the military camp on the right, turn right heading for Girne and Boğazköy. Within 3 miles (5km) there is a T-junction, turn left, there is a small petrol station (no unleaded).

Coming out of the village on the left is a restaurant where the *ayran* (yoghurt drink) is delicious. Sit under the ancient grapevine and try the *çorek*, a type of bread freshly baked on the premises.

Hilarion Route

Round trip approximately 1 ½ hours • 21 miles (34km)

This track is rough in places and is best driven in a jeep

Take the main road to Lefkoşa. As the road climbs through the mountain look to the right and the black silhouette figure is of **Kemal Atatürk**, the founder of modern day Turkey.

The road soon reaches a level plateau and a large picnic site is on the left. This is very popular with the locals especially during the warm summer nights. Begin to get into the right hand lane and just before the mountain pass there is a turning on the right at approximately 4 miles (6km). As you take this turning there is a large white 'fire prohibited' sign. This is the road to St Hilarion Castle.

This is an army controlled road, you must not stop or take photographs and you must keep to the tarmac route.

After negotiating the hairpin bend at 4.6 miles (7.4km) the Turkish Army Commando Camp is on the right. The road becomes narrow and windy after this point with wonderful views over Girne. The **war memorial** at 5.4 miles (8.7km) commemorates the soldiers from 1974. Directly after this is the **Lusignan Knight's jousting ground**, now used as a rifle range.

After another half a mile (1km) the road forks, for the mountain track bear left, the castle is straight on. Pull in at 6.8 miles (11km) for glorious views over the Mesaoria plain and Lefkoşa. At 7.8 miles (12.5km) the pine-clad plateau is a marvellous orchid area in the spring. Forest tracks cross over the main route at various different places, keep going straight.

The area becomes restricted at 8.3 miles (13.3km) and there is a sign here giving a warning. Just after this turn right. Do not be surprised to see an army sentry on this junction. There are army signs on either side of the road in red with the words 'ASKERİ BÖLGE' which translates to 'army zone' – do not enter. The restricted area finishes at 9.3 miles (14.9km) but it is not advisable to leave the track.

The track begins to descend and there are several deserted forestry buildings on the right. The views over the sea along this part of the route are stunning. At 13 miles (20.7km) turn right and at the next junction, 14 miles (23km), right again. **This part of the journey is very rough. An alternative route is to turn left and you will then join the beginning of 'Tank Route'.**

After half a mile (1km) turn left and at the next junction left again joining the tarmac road. At the bottom of the steep hill is a small perpetual waterfall. Follow the road to the village of **Malatya**. Drive straight through the village and the road descends for a mile (2km) to the village of **Alsancak**. Famous for its mountain water and citrus groves, there are some superb older buildings here. Drop down any road leading to the coast and turn right for Girne.

3
Gazimağusa (Famagusta)

Mağusa is the Turkish name for Gazimağusa and has been in use since the Ottoman conquest of 1571, *Gazi* means 'war veteran' or 'unconquered'. Gazimağusa is an ancient site and has a most impressive array of historical buildings.

HISTORY

The first settlement here is thought to have been circa 275BC, founded by Ptolemy Philadelphus of Egypt.

Arab chroniclers wrote with admiration of the booty taken from Cyprus and especially from Constantia (Salamis), which was destroyed in 648AD by the Emir Muawiya of Syria. The surviving inhabitants settled in the nearby, small lagoon town of Arsinoe, the present day Gazimağusa. The new immigrants renamed the town Ammochostos (hidden in sand) which was corrupted to Famagusta.

A royal city

For centuries Famagusta remained a small port. The Crusades stimulated the growth of the town into a

Above: The medieval Gothic cathedral of St Nicholas, now Lala Mustapha Paşa Mosque, in Gazimağusa

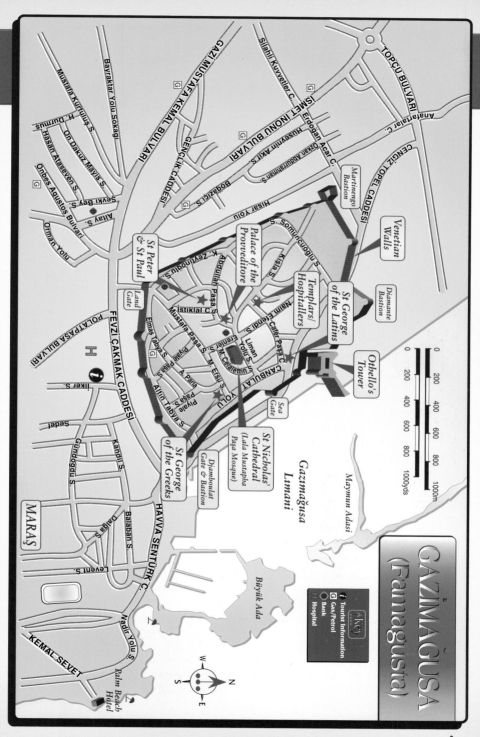

GAZIMAĞUSA (Famagusta)

TOPÇU BULVARI

CENGİZ TOPEL CADDESİ

Anafartalar C.

GAZİ MUSTAFA KEMAL BULVARI

İSMET İNÖNÜ BULVARI

Silahlı Kuvvetler C.

Erdoğan Acar C.

Hüseyin Akif S.

Özkan Abdurrahman S.

Boğaziçi S.

Hisar Yolu

Bayraklar Yolu Sokağı

Mustafa Kurtuluş S.

H. Durmuş

On Dakuz Mayis S.

Hasan Ataseven S.

Şevki Bey's S.

Altay S.

Onbeş Ağustos Bulvarı

Orman Yolu

GENÇLİK CADDESİ

S. Somuncuoğlu S.

K. Zeytinoğlu S.

Kısra S.

Abdullah Paşa S.

Naim Efendi S.

M. Cafer Paşa C.

Mustafa Paşa S.

Piyale Paşa S.

M. Ersoy S.

M. Celalettin S.

Liman Yolu S.

İstiklal C. S.

Elmas Tabya S.

Piyale Paşa S.

Altın Tabya S.

A. Paşa

CANBULAT YOLU

St Peter & St Paul

Land Gate

Palace of the Provveditore

Templars/Hospitallers

St George of the Latins

Venetian Walls

Diamante Bastion

Martinengo Bastion

Othello's Tower

Sea Gate

St Nicholas' Cathedral (Lala Mustapha Paşa Mosque)

Djamboulat Gate & Bastion

St George of the Greeks

Gazimağusa Limani

Maymun Adası

Büyük Ada

MARAŞ

FEVZİ ÇAKMAK CADDESİ

POLATPAŞA BULVARI

İlker S.

Sedef

Gündoğdu S.

Kandil S.

Balaban S.

Dalga S.

Levent S.

Nadir Yolu S.

HAVVA ŞENTÜRK C.

KEMAL SEVET

Palm Beach Hotel

Key

i Tourist Information
G Gas/Petrol
■ Bank
H Hospital

0 200 400 600 800 1000yds
0 200 400 600 800 1000m

W N E S

99

• Shopping in Gazimağusa •

Gazimagusa has been referred to as an 'outdoor museum' and this is an accurate description. The modern day shops rub shoulders with Lusignan and Venetian architecture.

A pedestrian area has recently been made in front of the Lala Mustapha Paşa mosque, (St Nicholas Cathedral) with benches to sit and watch the world go by. The main street is directly in front of the mosque with the usual selection of shops.

As you walk towards Othello's Tower from the mosque, the entrance to the small covered **market** is on the left. There is a wonderful selection of herbs and spices here. Turkish saffron is very reasonable. Opposite the covered market is a shop full of herbs and spices, they also sell flavoured teas, which are very popular on the mainland. Try a cup of the delicious apple tea, equally good hot or cold.

Further along the same road is **Esetik** the leather shop. Although, in general, leather is not a good buy here this shop does have a reasonable choice of jackets and handbags.

Next to Esetik is the delectable **Peteks Patisserie**. There are any number of sweet and savoury pastries; homemade ice cream and Turkish Delight to choose from. The toffee-like ice cream makes an excellent accompaniment to baklava. *Aşure* is a popular local speciality, consisting of fruit and wheat in a kind of syrup.

Gazimağusa has a branch of the **İş Bank**, with a cashpoint machine situated across the square from the mosque. Do not expect to find exchange bureaux.

major city. When the last stronghold of Christianity, Acre, fell in 1291 to the Saracens, there was a mass exodus of Christians from Syria and Palestine. The Lusignan King, Henry II, offered the fleeing refugees asylum at Famagusta. The town was fortified and made into a 'royal city' to compensate for what had been lost in the Holy Land.

The new settlers brought with them many skills as well as their wealth, which soon established Famagusta as one of the most im-

portant and wealthiest cities in the Levant. Cyprus became part of the trade route between Asia Minor and Egypt and Famagusta was regarded as the principal port of the Eastern Mediterranean. All of the major nations of the Mediterranean wanted a share of the wealth and established themselves here, as did military and religious orders.

The merchant traders and nobility were famous worldwide for their affluence; but this was all too short lived. With the dawn of the fifteenth century Lusignan power began to wane and the fabulous wealth of the island foundered. The rivalry of the two trading powers, Genoa and Venice overflowed, resulting in an event that marked the change of control.

During the coronation of Peter II, in 1373AD a serious riot broke out in Famagusta. Traditionally a nobleman from each of the courts of Genoa and Venice would walk beside the monarch at his Coronation. An argument erupted as to which side each would take and the resulting fight turned into a massacre which propelled Genoa to send armies to take the island by storm. This it did, sacking Nicosia (Lefkoşa), Kyrenia (Girne) and Bellapais, and held Famagusta for more than a century. Isolated from the rest of Cyprus, the wealthy population left and so followed a rapid decline in the prosperity of the city. By the time the Venetians took over Cyprus in 1489, the city was half-empty.

As with Lefkoşa and Girne, the Venetians undertook major rebuilding work. The invention of gunpowder rendered the Lusignan defences obsolete. The Venetians reconstructed the citadel which guards the harbour and built massive walls guarded by bastions, encircling the town.

Seige of the last Christian outpost

When the Ottoman forces arrived in 1570 they quickly took Nicosia (Lefkoşa) and Kyrenia (Girne). Famagusta (Gazimağusa) remained the last Christian outpost in the east. The ten-month siege that followed was a bitter one with much ferocity and heroism on both sides. With the improved defences, the Venetians under Marc Antonio Bragadino held out for ten months. Hunger and a lack of supplies were serious problems for the troops inside the walls. There were only 8,000 Venetians to the Ottoman force of some 200,000.

Venice did not send the promised help and the Turks built enormous earthworks around the walls, which enabled them to fire their cannonballs into the city with greater accuracy. One hundred thousand cannonballs are said to have landed, some can still be seen today. On August 1st 1571, the Venetians surrendered. There was not a cat, rat or feathered creature left to eat.

Bragadino, who had signed the terms of honourable surrender, was imprisoned, tortured, then flayed alive. His skin was stuffed with straw and paraded around the city as a trophy of conquest. The Turks said that he had been killed because he had not kept to the terms of surrender, a charge that was trumped up and totally false.

The Turks did very little with Gazimağusa. The city was used as a prison for dissidents and those who had offended the Sultan. Many buildings were demolished in the mid-nineteenth century to provide material for works at Port Said and the Suez Canal.

Construction of the Cyprus Government Railway began from Gazimağusa and the first section of the line to Lefkoşa was opened in October 1905. This did not last long. The last train journey from Lefkoşa to Gazimağusa was on 31st December 1951. At its peak the 'CGR' had twelve locomotives, twenty-four freight cars and six passenger coaches.

The Venetian walls

The huge walls which fortify the city, up to 50ft (15m) high and 25ft (7.6m) thick, are interspersed with bastions throughout the perimeter with a major bastion at each corner. The designer Giovanni Sanmichele did not live to see his ideas completed, dying of a fever in 1559. There were originally two entrances to the city, the Land Gate and the Sea Gate.

The **Land Gate** is guarded by a ravelin and was entered by a draw-bridge. When the ravelin was breached by the invading Ottoman forces, the Venetians retaliated by blowing it up, resulting in massive loss of Turkish life. The present Land Gate entrance into the old city is by way of a solid bridge built by the Otto-mans after their conquest. Left and right of the entrance arch are the 'cavaliers', ramps up which the can-nons were drawn by horse to fire from the gunnery platforms above.

TOUR OF THE CITY

Ramparts walk

There is a walk along the ramparts with delightful views over the city. There are four minor bastions located along the south-west wall, culminating in the **Martinengo Bastion**, which is considered to be one of the finest examples of mili-tary architecture of the sixteenth century, and was the masterpiece of the Venetian restructuring. This

The ravelin, bastion that guards the land gate to the old city of Famagusta

Above: Pedestrianised forecourt to the Palace of the Provveditore, with the church of the Franciscans behind

Below: Inside the Lala Mustapha Pasa Mosque

collected the adjacent walls into a huge spearhead. The Ottomans regarded it as impregnable, and did not attempt to assault it. Two huge underground vaults were discovered here, their purpose is not clear, but maybe the Venetians used them for military stores. The north-eastern corner was defended by the **Diamante Bastion**.

Othello's Tower

The harbour was guarded by **The Citadel**, now called Othello's Tower. The Citadel was originally built by the Lusignans in the fourteenth century to defend the entrance to the harbour. It is rectangular with a square tower offset at each corner and was surrounded by a moat. The Venetians reconstructed the citadel in 1492 for use as an artillery stronghold. The upper floor was

Othello, the Moor of Venice

The British renamed The Citadel 'Othello's Tower' due to the connection of Cyprus with Shakespeare's *Othello*, although the playwright had only mentioned a 'sea port in Cyprus'.

Othello, the Moor of Venice has been identified with a Venetian Governor of Cyprus, Christophoro Moro, whose surname means 'Moor'. He was in Cyprus from 1506 to 1508 and it is known that he returned to Venice without his wife. Could she have been the model for the tragic Desdemona?

removed to fit in with the height of the great wall and remodelled with round towers. The walls were widened by approximately 20ft (6m) in places.

There are two models in the custodian's office. The first shows the building as it was originally designed by the French and the second one shows the changes made by the Venetians.

Over the main **entrance** door to the citadel there is a marble slab, carved with the winged lion of St Mark, the name of the Prefect of Cyprus Nicolo Foscarini and the date 1942. The entrance leads into a square Frankish tower which leads into the **courtyard**. Upon entering the courtyard, the well-preserved fourteenth century **refectory** is through a door on the opposite side of the court with the large kitchen at one end. Tall Gothic arches support the vaulted roof. The windows were kept small for defence purposes and were blocked up on the harbour side by the Venetians.

To the right of the refectory, a doorway opens into a chamber from which the **gun ports** of the present north-east tower may be reached. The passage is dark and a torch is necessary. There are some interesting examples of old cannon, both Venetian and Ottoman lying on the floor near the refectory door, and there is a collection of cannonballs kept in the citadel, most made of cast iron. The large stone balls were used as missiles for the 'trebuchet', a huge catapult.

Steps lead up to the battlements where there is a fine view of the city and harbour.

Please be aware that there is a military post here, with a red warning sign, forbidding photography in their area.

In medieval times the harbour had a huge iron chain which could be drawn across the entrance as a defence system, and opposite the citadel can be seen a clump of rocks on a promontory where the chain tower used to stand. The remains of former apartments for the nobility are evident with fireplaces and window seats, which give a fine view over the court.

The Sea Gate

To the south of the tower is **Porta del Mare or Sea Gate**. This elegant gate was built by Nicolo Prioli in 1496 and at time of writing is being restored. The portcullis, which guards the harbour entrance, is still in place.

To one side of the gate is a large limestone sculpture of a lion. According to legend this benign looking creature is supposed to open his mouth and roar on one day of the year. Anyone who is near enough and brave enough to put his hand into the lion's mouth will reap untold riches.

Djamboulat's Gate

Continuing southward towards the **Djamboulat or Arsenal Gate and Bastion**, scant remains of ruined churches can be seen.

At the arched entrance next to the bastion the Venetians had erected a fiendish machine, a wheel covered with knives. If ever an invader tried to force their way through the entrance the blades would cut them to pieces. During one battle, the Ottoman General Djamboulat grew despondent on seeing how many of his men had been killed and decided to take

drastic action. He rode his horse straight into the deadly machine. He and his mount were killed immediately, but he achieved his mission, the apparatus was brought to a halt and access to the city was gained.

It is said that his spirit urged the Ottomans on, and wherever the fighting was at its worst his ghost appeared. He is buried in the bastion where he gave his life and his **tomb** and a small **museum** are there. From here the wall leads back to the Land Gate past the four minor supporting bastions.

If walking the walls be aware that there are many unguarded openings and rickety balustrades.

St Nicholas' Cathedral
(Lala Mustapha Paşa Mosque)

The former cathedral is the most impressive and important monument in Gazimağusa. It was here that the Lusignan kings were crowned *in absentia* as kings of Jerusalem after they had been crowned as kings of Cyprus in Nicosia at St Sophia.

In 1472 James II married Caterina Cornaro in St Nicholas and it was here, seventeen years later that the widowed Caterina signed her abdication, thereby ending the Lusignan Dynasty. James II and his infant son James III, who was born posthumously, the last sovereigns of the Lusignan line are buried here. The cathedral was soon turned into a mosque by the Ottomans and initially called Aysofya Cami, later changed to Lala Mustapha Paşa Mosque, after the Ottoman General who conquered Cyprus.

(cont'd on page 109)

ST BARNABAS:

Getting there

To get to St Barnabas from Girne, follow the main Lefkoşa-Gazimağusa road. Approximately 4 miles (7km) before Gazimağusa there is a signpost to the left for Salamis. Follow this through the village of Mutluyaka and take the next left signposted St Barbabas. The monastery is 500 yards (460m) on the left.

From Gazimağusa take the Boğaz road. Two miles (3km) outside the town turn left at the St Barnabas signpost. Pass the Royal Tombs on the left and St Barnabas is 200 yards (180m) on the right.

The dream

"As they were ministered to the Lord, and fasted, the Holy Ghost said separate me, "Barnabas and Saul for the work whereunto I have called them". And when they had fasted and prayed, and laid their hands on them, they sent them away. So they, being sent forth by the Holy Ghost, departed unto Seleucia; and from thence they sailed to Cyprus. And when they were at Salamis, they preached the word of God in the synagogues of the Jews; and they had also John to their minister." – ACTS XIII.

After the remarkable dream of Archbishop Anthemios, when the remains of St Barnabas were revealed to him, the Emperor Zeno granted autocephalous status to the church of Cyprus and gave ample funds to build a church on the site where the sepulchre was found. A hospice for pilgrims and a shrine for St Barnabas was also erected.

In 1991 the Antiquities Department opened up the monastic buildings as an **Icon and Archaeological Museum**. The church underwent a full restoration programme, the gardens were landscaped to include a fountain in the middle and the cloisters now house the archaeological artefacts.

The monastery

The present day building dates from 1756 and the white domes are a local landmark. Into the walls have been incorporated some of the early Byzantine capitals and pillars. In the right hand alcove facing the altar there is a spirally

(cont'd overleaf)

One of the many exquisite examples of ancient pottery in the St Barnabas archaeological museum

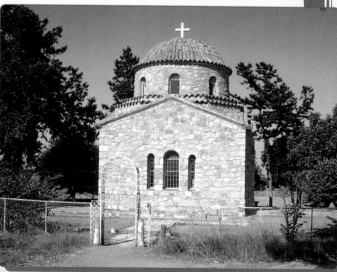

Right: The nineteenth century mausoleum above the tomb of St Barnabas

Opposite: The monastery church of St Barnabas, now an Icon museum

ST BARNABAS: MONASTERY, ICON & ARCHAEOLOGICAL MUSEUM

(cont'd from previous page)

carved pillar, which is reputed to ooze a healing unguent. The continual touching of pilgrims' hands has left part of the pillar black and smooth.

There is a life-size fresco to the right of the entrance to the church. This was painted by three brother priests, Chariton, Barnabas and Stephanos who lived and worked at St Barnabas. Not only brothers in the church but brothers in blood. Their mother is buried beneath the tree within the monastery precinct, close to what is now the café.

The fresco shows the dream of Anthemios, and depicts him finding the sepulchre under the carob tree containing the remains of St Barnabas and a copy of St Matthew's Gospel in St Barnabas' own handwriting.

The central scene is set in the courtyard of the Imperial Chapel of St Stephen in Constantinople. Anthemios with other Cypriot clergy gives The Gospel to the Byzantine Emperor Zeno. Zeno confers the imperial privileges on Anthemios. These were that the Church of Cyprus was to be independent and the Archbishop may sign in red ink, wear a cope of imperial purple and carry an imperial sceptre like the Byzantine emperors. These customs have been maintained to this day.

Many of the other icons on display were also painted by the brothers. One would sketch and outline, one fill in the broad colours and the other would complete the details. This division of labour was to help cope with the demand from people placing orders.

The Archaeological Museum

The well laid out Archaeological Museum in the cloisters has many artefacts from Neolithic to Roman times. There are some superb Bronze Age specimens, and the items within the museum cover the 9,000 years of Cyprus' history.

Tomb of St Barnabas

A short distance from the monastic buildings is the tomb of the Apostle, near the eucalyptus trees. It is here that Archbishop Anthemios found the relics of St Barnabas. The steps down to the tomb are rough and uneven and the lighting minimal. The mausoleum over the tomb was built in the nineteenth century and became one of the principal places of pilgrimage of the Orthodox Christians.

The tomb of St Barnabas is still a place of pilgrimage for Greek Cypriots who live in the north. The Saint's Day is June 11th.

What to see in the cathedral

Although St Nicholas does not have the scale of decoration that St Sophia in Lefkoşa has, it is far more elegantly proportioned. The western façade has three large porches, with elaborately carved canopies above and a splendid **rose window**. This is the best preserved and most impressive part of the building. The **carving** on the statue canopies and brackets is truly outstanding. The statues have long since been lost but their tiny vaulted canopies, decorated with finials and crockets are spectacular. The cathedral was badly damaged during the siege of 1571, including most of its flying buttresses and the twin towers.

There is a central nave with two aisles, side chapels, and a triple apse. Two rows of columns support the vaulting over the nave and aisles. The architecture tends to be solid because of the risk of earthquakes. There are fine lancet and rosette windows in the apse.

The domed building in the forecourt or *parvis*, used to be a **Medrese** (Moslem religious school) and opposite is a sixteenth century Venetian building now used for ablutions. It has a finely carved arched doorway and two circular windows surmounted by Venetian coats of arms. The long marble frieze to the left of the doorway is from Salamis. The enormous tree is a sycamore fig (*Ficus sycomorus*), approximately six hundred years old.

French palace and courtyard

Opposite St Nicholas is the **Palazzo del Provveditore**, the remains of the Lusignan Palace. Ruined by an earthquake in the sixteenth century, it was the residence of the Kings of Cyprus until 1369. The façade, with four granite columns from Salamis, is a Venetian addition and the central arch bears the arms of Giovanni Renier, Governor of Cyprus in 1552. Part of the palace was later used as a prison during the Ottoman era, one of the detainees being the poet and playwright Namik Kemal. The Sultan disliked his progressive ideas and views and he was deported in 1873 to Gazimağusa where he spent 38 months in exile. His prison is now a **museum** in his memory. His bronze bust facing the square named after him was erected in 1953.

Church of St Peter and St Paul

To the south-west lies the **Church of St Peter and St Paul**. Built by a rich merchant during the reign of Peter I, with a fraction of the proceeds of a single consignment shipped to Syria. Flying buttresses support the vaulting of the nave. In 1571 the damage of the bombardment was repaired, the church was restored and converted to a mosque and renamed Sinan Paşa Mosque. During British rule it was used to store products such as wheat, hence the popular name 'Wheat Mosque'. In 1964 it was restored again and eventually the Ministry of Education took it over and it is now the public library.

(cont'd on page 112)

• Marine Turtles •

In 1991, the Society for the Protection of Turtles in Northern Cyprus (SPoT) organised a student expedition from Glasgow University to conduct a survey of the nesting beaches around the north coast. This has developed into an on-going project and now involves students from more than ten universities, with volunteers from eight nations.

There are at least seven species of marine turtles world-wide today. The loggerhead (*caretta caretta*) and the green (*chelonia mydas*) turtles are found in Cyprus. Marine turtles begin their lives on land where they emerge from the nest after forty to sixty days' incubation in the sand. They head off towards the sea, guided by both the slope of the beach and visual cues. It is thought that they spend the next three to five years in offshore waters feeding on pelagic invertebrates and algae, although little is known of these 'lost years'. It is estimated that only one hatchling in two thousand will survive to maturity at twenty to thirty years of age.

During the nesting season females will lay between one to ten clutches of eggs. They may nest roughly every one to three years. Recent advances in genetic techniques are backing the theory that marine turtles lay on the same beach on which they were hatched.

In Northern Cyprus the turtles nest between May and August. Hatching starts mid-July and continues until mid-October. The students conduct daytime surveys of some forty nesting beaches around the island, recording activities and any threats, such as foxes and dogs digging up the nest and eating the eggs. The turtles are tagged, and the data collected shows that in a good year there are approximately 150 green turtles and 180 loggerhead turtles nesting on the beaches of Northern Cyprus.

Of the total of 400 nests recorded in 1996, between June 11 and July 31, 46.8 per cent hatched, 20.3 per cent suffered from predators, 12.8 per cent were inundated by the sea, and for 20.3 per cent the fate is unknown.

In July 1998 three green turtles were fitted with a tracking device. This is providing vital information on the habits of the turtles and the distances and areas to which they travel. However it is an expensive project and relies totally on funding by voluntary donations.

Adopt a turtle

The main base is at **Alagadi beach**, this is where nightly surveys of nesting females are conducted and the turtles are tagged. The students welcome visits from visitors hoping to see their 'own' nesting turtle. It is a good idea to contact the students in the daytime to arrange a time with them. It is possible to adopt a turtle. For more information please contact:

Annette Broderick and Brendan Godley, Marine Turtle Research Group,
School of Biological Sciences,
University of Wales,
Singleton Park,
Swansea
SA2 8PP
e-mail: MTN@swan.ac.uk
Web site:
www.seaturtle.org/mtrg/

Society for the Protection of Turtles in Northern Cyprus (SpoT)
PO Box 42
Girne
Mersin. 10
Turkey

Turtle Beach east of Girne with wire-shelters for the turtle nests

Historic churches

To the north of the recently constructed square in front of the cathedral is Kişla Sokak, once lined with the luxurious houses of the Lusignan nobility.

This road brings you to the twin churches of the **Knights Templar** and the **Hospitallers**. Both are fourteenth century structures. The larger of the two was built by the Templars and dedicated to St Anthony. When the Pope dissolved the order in 1313 the church was taken over by the Hospitallers.

Near to St Nicholas are the lofty ruins of the **church of St George of the Greeks**. This large, unique church was once the Orthodox Cathedral and combines both Gothic and Byzantine elements in its structure. Only three walls have survived and there are fragments of fifteenth century painting in the apses. The church was badly damaged during the Ottoman bombardment which caused the roof to collapse. There are still cannonballs to be seen, lodged in the masonry of the west wall.

St George of the Latins is just south of Othello's Tower. There is evidence that this church was fortified and therefore built before any city walls. Traces of a crenellated parapet remain and a watchtower on the north-west corner. There are claims that the church was built from the remains of a classic temple at Salamis. Although the carved capitals are eroded, foliar motifs and an unusual design depicting winged dragons can be made out. Only the north door has survived, but there was also an entrance on the south and to the west.

The tall, elegant stature of this church is still evident from the remaining north wall and polygonal choir. Its large, slender windows once contained fine Gothic tracery. The gargoyles, regrettably all beheaded, are many and varied, among them a naked kneeling man, a robed figure and an eagle. To the right of the north doorway there is a carving of a bearded figure and a carving of a lion with the head of a sheep or a donkey in its mouth. Somehow these two carvings, both representations abhorred by the Ottomans, escaped being mutilated.

There are many more ruins of churches and ancient buildings in Gazimağusa. Look out for the **marble fountains** around the city, some still in use, and the **Turkish Baths**, easily identified by the domed roofs.

Maraş/Varosha

The once prosperous suburb of Maraş or Varosha, now lies behind the Atilla line (the border which divides the country) and is easily visible from the Palm Beach Hotel. It is an expanse of hotels and flats, built in the late 1960s and early 1970s. Much of it lines the sandy shore for which this area is so famous. It was extremely popular with tourists, and anyone visiting Cyprus in the early 1970s would probably have stayed in this area. Due to the political stalemate it remains in the hands of the Turkish Cypriot authorities. It is strictly forbidden to photograph any part of this area.

BEACHES IN THE GAZIMAĞUSA AREA

Gazimağusa has long been famous for its miles of sandy beaches. Before 1974 it was a very popular tourist resort. Unfortunately Golden Sands beach now lies behind the Attila line but there are many other beaches to enjoy.

The Palm Beach Hotel looks out over a delightful sandy beach, which the hotel maintains to a high standard. The entrance fee entitles you to use the sun loungers, sunshades, showers and toilets. A snack bar serves food, drinks and ice cream throughout the day. Turtles are commonly seen in this area during the height of the summer season.

Leaving Gazimağusa take the signs for **Salamis**, turning right at the roundabout with the large black peace statue, 'The Monument to Victory'. About 4 miles (6.4km) from this roundabout is the Golden Terrace restaurant. A track here leads down to **Glapsides Beach**. This is a popular sandy beach with beach bar. Sunshades and sun loungers are very limited.

A superb walk (3.7 miles/6km), along the sand takes you to the next beach along, known as **Silver Beach**. Situated at the far south of the Salamis ruins, this is a great spot for swimming and snorkelling. The sand shelves slowly making it safe for children. It is most interesting to explore the now submerged harbour of the ancient city. There are no facilities here.

The main entrance for Salamis is well signposted off the main road. At the entrance is **Salamis Beach**. Another lovely soft sandy beach with limited facilities. A cooling swim is most welcome after the heat of walking around Salamis.

Follow the main road heading east towards the Karpas Peninsula. A twenty-minute drive from Salamis is **Kocak Restaurant**. This is situated on a very pleasant sandy beach with sunshades and sun loungers. Whilst there is no fee to use the beach you are expected to purchase refreshments from the restaurant.

As you continue along the main road you will pass **Mimoza Hotel** and **Cyprus Gardens**. Each of these accommodations has a sandy beach with full facilities. Both beaches are generally busy with their residents.

4

Salamis

Without doubt the most important and fascinating site in Northern Cyprus, Salamis was founded around the twelfth century BC and had a long and mostly affluent development until its destruction by Arab raiders, earthquake and tidal waves in the seventh century. It is a large city complex that has been partially excavated to reveal wonders of Roman buildings and engineering.

The remains of the city are situated on the east coast, north of Gazimağusa and are well signposted from whichever direction they are approached.

HISTORY OR LEGEND?

What little is known about the early remains of Salamis relies mostly on legend. It is believed that Teucer founded a settlement here at the end of the Trojan War. He is thought to have fallen out with his father, Telamon, who banished him from his homeland.

After landing on the northern shores on the beach of the Achaens, Teucer and his followers crossed the Karpas Peninsula and founded a township at the mouth of the Pedios River. Teucer named the town

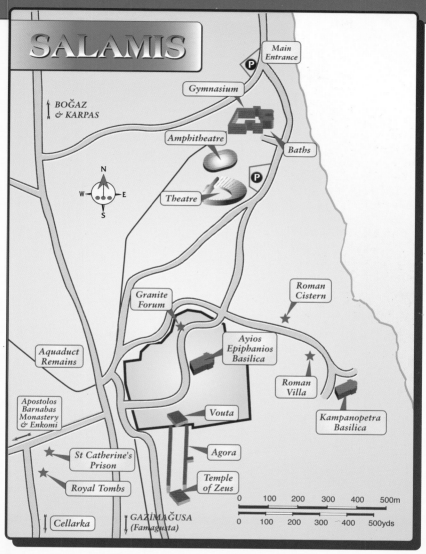

SALAMIS

Main Entrance

Gymnasium

BOĞAZ & KARPAS

Amphitheatre

Baths

N
W — E
S

Theatre

Granite Forum

Roman Cistern

Aquaduct Remains

Ayios Epiphanios Basilica

Roman Villa

Apostolos Barnabas Monastery & Enkomi

Vouta

Kampanopetra Basilica

St Catherine's Prison

Agora

Royal Tombs

Temple of Zeus

| 0 | 100 | 200 | 300 | 400 | 500m |

| 0 | 100 | 200 | 300 | 400 | 500yds |

Cellarka

GAZİMAĞUSA (Famagusta)

Salamis after the island of his birth. There was probably little development until around 1200BC when the inhabitants of the nearby city of **Enkomi** discovered that their harbour was silting up and it was essential to find new access for shipping if the copper exports were not to suffer. Salamis was the nearest and most logical place to develop.

Before the eighth century BC Salamis was the most important

commercial centre on the island and by the sixth century BC was being referred to in ancient texts with regard to the payment of taxes to the Assyrian overlords.

Attempted revolt against the Persian rulers failed and it was not until Alexander the Great demolished the might of the Persian Empire in 334BC that stability returned to the island.

The Empire of Alexander spread far, and after his death the governing powers of Cyprus were the Hellenistic dynasty ruling Egypt, the Ptolemys. However there were still kings in each of the island's city kingdoms and the last king of Salamis, Nicocreon, fought against the armies of Ptolemy only to be vanquished and forced to commit suicide along with his entire family around 295BC.

Pax Romana

The Roman period which began in 58BC brought peace, a stability that was not interrupted by revolt or war, and with it came an upsurge in commerce. The Romans developed Salamis into a city displaying all the evidence of prosperity. They also increased trading, enlarging the harbour which is situated to the south of the main city buildings.

Development of the city was hampered by earthquakes which caused considerable damage in the first and fourth centuries.

Due to the conversion of Barnabas, a native Salamis Jew to Christianity, the city became a centre for Christian teaching and there was a large Christian community here long before that faith was officially recognised as the religion of the Roman Empire. In fact the spread of Christianity was so rapid that the Jewish community felt threatened by it and revolted with horrifying results in 110AD. It is reported that 250,000 Christians were slaughtered by the Jews, resulting in the Roman army putting down the revolt and expelling all Jews from the island.

It is obvious from the remains visible today that Salamis was built very much with leisure and pleasure to the forefront of the architect's design. The city was rebuilt and renamed Constantia in the fourth century after the architect of the rebuilding, the Emperor Constantius II. It is evident in every piece of wall still standing and held in place by reinforcing buttresses, that the Romans did not want to lose their once powerful city and move away towards the south.

One part of the city entertainment facilities, definitely not rebuilt, was the theatre. Much of the stone and marble flooring from the fifty-tiered theatre was taken away and used in the rebuilding of the bath houses.

Decline and death

Never again did Salamis regain its former glory. The harbour silted up, forcing trade south to what is now Gazimağusa and the other ports of Larnaca and Limassol.

Earthquake and tidal wave plus the Arab raids of the seventh century sounded the final death knell for Salamis and for many hundreds of years thereafter the city remains rested under the sands that had engulfed them.

However, successive civilisations living and ruling on Cyprus have all plundered the site for building materials: marble sarcophagi for decorative purposes, granite, marble columns and the mosaics that once would have graced the walkways, now not a trace of these is apparent.

In the modern world we call the removal of artefacts for use elsewhere, recycling, and this is how the visitor has to view the dispersal of items from Salamis. Fortunately many of the items recycled are still very much in evidence today. For example the two marble sarcophagi at Bellapais, and the four granite columns that form the facade of the palace of the Provveditore in Gazimağusa.

A TOUR OF SALAMIS

A tour of the entire site will take a couple of days and much patience. It is difficult to find some of the places that are marked on the maps, because, for the last twenty-five years, there have been no archaeological expeditions on the island. The result of this neglect is plainly seen. All the cleared areas which were not of immediate interest and therefore have not been much visited have now been taken over by nature. The thorny 'Duke of Argyll's tea tree', mimosa and giant fennel present a lavish display of colour in springtime and make the site as fascinating botanically as historically.

On entering the site from the Salamis Bay gateway, the **bath house** complex, **amphitheatre** and **theatre** are on the right. It is this part of the complex that is the most visited and access to most of it is fairly clear.

There is a large parking area at the rear of the theatre and from this point the visitor has a panoramic view of the rear theatre wall, the barely identifiable amphitheatre outline, the colonnaded street leading to the gymnasium and bath houses.

The theatre

Starting with the theatre, entrance is gained through what would have been a tunnel leading into the **auditorium**. The **orchestra**, which was originally paved with marble, is approximately 85ft (26m) in diameter and the **proscenium or stage** is 120ft (37m) wide. At the rear of the stage is a vast complex of **dressing rooms**. These are now extremely difficult to reach as the mimosa and giant fennel grow in profusion. The best view can be obtained from the top tier of the auditorium.

The seating arrangements of the theatre are now less than half the original and the extant structure is the work of the archaeologists. There are now nineteen tiers divided into sections by eight rows of steps. The central sector was obviously used by the city's rulers, as is evident from the deeper seating arrangement. Before destruction by the earthquake in the fourth century the theatre had forty to fifty tiers for the audience. That part of the theatre not reconstructed was supported by buttresses, the perimeter of these is plainly visible at the rear of the solid wall.

As this venue for dramatic performance was built before the dawn of Christianity, there would have been statues of pagan gods and goddesses lining the stage area and a small sacrifice would have been made to appease the gods before every performance. The piece of marble column and the carved pediment in the centre of the auditorium have been placed there in recent years to represent the **sacrificial block**.

The amphitheatre

Leaving the theatre and heading for the **colonnaded street**, the amphitheatre is on the left. It is possible to see the remains of the tiers for the seating and there are a few column stumps remaining. The pits that were being dug and the contents sifted with great care by the archaeologists are to the forefront revealing some of the retaining wall.

It is not worth more than a cursory view of the amphitheatre because as with so much of the site, after twenty-five years of neglect the undergrowth has taken a very strong upper hand.

The street

To the right of the colonnaded street there is a building with a barrel-vaulted roof. This was one of the **cisterns** of the city and this one provided the water for the bath houses and the swimming pools. The southern wall of this structure has an area of tiered seating. Again there is a section with deeper seats, which leads to the supposition that here must have been an area for some sort of performance. Various theories as to its use include: a small odeon for musical recital, or an area in which the athletes were examined before competing in the amphitheatre.

The columns of the colonnaded street would originally have been of

One of the few mosaic remnants of Salamis. This is a representation of Apollo and his sister Artemis slaying the children of Niobe

The gymnasium square, surrounded by the marble columns of the 'stoa'

limestone, plastered and painted. The street would have been covered with a tiled roof.

The marble pieces of column used in the reconstruction of the entrance have been brought from different parts of the site.

The gymnasium

On reaching the top of the street, the view over the **gymnasium** is one of the most dramatic vistas at Salamis, especially in the springtime, when it is bedecked with flowers.

Once again the marble columns surrounding the square court that was the exercise ground of the gymnasts, are not in their original place. These have been brought from basilicas and temples around the site to create the balanced perspective of an imposing gymnasium surrounded by a covered walkway or *stoa*. This had leading off it various rooms, which would have served as shops, meeting places, etc.

Apart from the very evident modern recycling of materials in the reconstruction of this area, there is also evidence of previous recycling. Pieces of broken limestone column feature frequently in the walls of this complex along with fragments of fine carvings. It is also evident that the two **swimming pools** at the north and south end of the eastern section of the stoa were originally round. After the fourth century rebuild they were made rectangular.

The south-western corner of the stoa contains the **latrines**, with seating for forty-four persons. An area that once was open with a clear view of the gymnasium was blocked by a wall when Christianity came to the city. The washing and flushing system of the latrines is clearly visible.

The floor of the gymnasium is a profusion of different patterns and colours of opus sectile tiling. Unfortunately large sections have disappeared and what remains is being damaged by the roots of wild shrubs growing in its midst. There has been no proper repair to the opus sectile since 1974 and the incursion of more thick rooted plants can only cause continual serious damage. The multi-coloured wild flowers of springtime do little harm and soon die back in the withering heat of summer.

Statues

Continuing round the walkway the visitor will arrive at the swimming pool in the north-east corner. The pool is surrounded by statues that came from the theatre. With the exception of one, they are all headless, and female. There is one tall toga'd male godlike figure. He too is headless but much larger than the robed female figures. The figure retaining a head but no face is a representation of the Goddess Persephone, the Queen of Darkness or Night, hence she has been carved in black marble. Her face would have been of a different coloured marble, as would her hands. Heads and hands of statues throughout the transitional periods of paganism to Christianity to Islam have all suffered in the name of religious fanaticism.

Bath houses

There are two entrances to the bath houses from the eastern stoa, both lead into a chamber containing an octagonal *frigidarium*. This pool would have been constantly filled with icy water and the user would then go through into a small heated antechamber before entering the main central *sudatorium*, or sweating room. Remains of the *hypocaust* (underfloor heating) system can be seen.

In the arch of the southern doorway to the sudatorium are the remains of a sixth century fresco depicting a scene from one of the exploits of Hercules. In this picture Hercules' friend, Hylas, is seen refusing the temptation of the water nymph. Doorways in the eastern wall lead to a large chamber in the apse of which there is a hot water bath, or *caldarium*; beneath the floor of this is the furnace area. In a partly closed up wall niche of this chamber is one of the few remaining mosaic fragments.

This entire complex of chambers which make up the remaining area of sudatoria extends to the north of the chamber containing the caldarium and there is another fragmentary mosaic to be seen in the arched embrasure of the northern wall (the buttresses erected in the fourth century rebuild are plainly visible). From this room, exit is effected through another octagonal frigidarium into the eastern walk of the stoa.

From the swimming pool surrounded by statues there is a doorway that leads to the outside of the bath houses on the north side and a small set of **public latrines** with a remarkably intact opus sectile floor.

All round the perimeter from the north walls the water channel that led from the south-easterly cistern of the complex can be seen. Now much buckled and distorted by time and earthquake disturbance. This channel would have once supplied the water for the latrines, the swimming pool and frigidarium of the northern section.

There are two more pieces of wall mosaic to be seen and they are to be found in the area largely below at the apsidal end of the sudatorium.

These depict the river god, Eurotas, whose bearded face can be plainly seen as can one white feathered wing of a swan. Further down the incline and well-protected from the elements is a mosaic which depicts Apollo and his twin sister Artemis slaying Niobe's children. A pair of strong manly legs, a quiver of arrows and a shield are all that remain of the main representation. The face in the lower frieze which has an air of sadness about it could possibly be that of the grieving mother.

OTHER PARTS OF SALAMIS

There are other excavated areas on the site and if time permits an attempt to see some of them will be worth the effort.

Follow the map and from the rear of the theatre take the left fork in the road as far as the crossroads. Here turn left and carry on until a corrugated iron roof can be seen on the right. There is a rusty sign that states it is an old mill. Here are the remains of a **Roman villa**, which was adapted for industrial use after the city lost its commercial prominence.

Returning to the main track continue with the sea on the left until there is a branch in the road. Turn left and on the right can be seen the remaining marble pillars of the **Kampanopetra basilica**. Built around the fourth century there are three aisles and two side passages. In the south passage there are marble sarcophagi.

At the eastern end of the main basilica is another group of buildings with an *atrium* and below these rooms at a much lower level are the remains of a **water cistern** and a small **bath house**. The entrance hall to the baths contains a very fine piece of opus sectile flooring which has an exquisite geometrical pattern.

On a hot day at this point, the sea will be very tempting and the swimming here is highly recommended.

To view more of the site return to the crossroads leaving the oil mill on the left. Turn left and slowly follow the road. There are some massive **granite columns** toppled among the undergrowth on the right and opposite them on the left of the road just visible through the weeds can be seen the perfect circular surround of what was possibly a **well** for public use (some guidebooks refer to it as a water clock).

Ayios Epiphanios Basilica

Follow the road until the fenced off area that is the basilica built by Epiphanios when he was Bishop of Salamis towards the end of the fourth century. This is the largest purpose-built Christian basilica known on Cyprus and measures 190 by 135ft (58 by 41m).

The remains of the building are not impressive and there is little to see. The archaeologists have placed stumps of column, identifying the aisles. In the south-east section of the basilica are the remains of a hypocaust system to warm the water for the baptismal font.

The bones of St Epiphanios once resided in the tomb in the southern apse. From there according to conflicting report they were removed either to St Simeon in Gazimağusa

• ENKOMI •

The next site linked with Salamis is Enkomi and this is reached from the Royal Tombs area, passing the monastery of St Barnabas on the right. At the next junction turn right, the entrance to the city is almost immediately on the left.

History

The city was renowned throughout the trade routes for its copper smelting and exports from its ancient harbour, no trace of which now remains. There is little to show save for the city foundations. These were laid out on a grid system, and it is a fascinating area to explore, preferably in early winter when all the vegetation has died back and the outline of the city streets can be plainly seen.

First discovered in 1896, the excavators' initial findings were of burials. Believing that this was just an extension of the Salamis necropolis they left the site and it was not until the 1930s that Enkomi was explored again. It was during these digs that the outline of the city began to emerge and so revealed the customs of the people. The burial of the dead within the courtyards of the houses is the Mycenaean custom and evidence of this type of ritual has been found in Mycenae and Crete.

Archaeological findings date Enkomi to approximately 2000BC and for many years it was thought that Enkomi was the Alasia referred to in the text found on the cuneiform tablets discovered on the site of Tell el-Amarna in Egypt. These were inscribed in the mid-fourteenth century BC and are a diplomatic correspondence between foreign powers.

or to Constantinople, maybe to both?

Water cistern

Follow the road leading away from the basilica and it bears off to the right with a track joining it from the left. Just beyond this junction the impressive walls of the *vouta*, or the water cistern, can be seen on the left.

The water to fill this cistern, which provided Salamis with continual running water, was carried across the Mesaoria plain on an aqueduct 35 miles (56 km) long. The source of the water was a perpetual spring in the Beşparmak mountains at Kythrea (Değirmenlik) which still flows today. The water for the city was carried by short lengths of terracotta piping joined by limestone mortar. Forced by sheer water pressure from the huge mass of water in the cistern it could be taken to any part of the city.

It is believed to be the largest above-ground water cistern to be found anywhere throughout the

Some doubt, due to microscopic analysis of the tablets, has now been shed on the true identity of Alasia as there is some evidence that it could be a site south of the Troodos Mountains. Verification has yet to be provided but there is no doubt that Enkomi was an extremely powerful city and continued to be so until

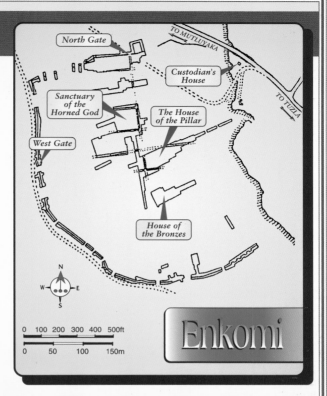

the harbour silted up. At this time around 1200BC the inhabitants moved a couple of miles away to help swell the population of Salamis and continue the development of their commercial enterprises.

Roman Empire and consists of a huge vaulted chamber, the roof of which was supported by thirty-six large square pillars placed in three rows. The massively strong corbels that carried the roof vaulting can be plainly seen along the walls.

Also visible are the sluices that fed into chambers on the south wall. These chambers filled with water, performed the task of buttresses and in turn fed the ornamental water system that decorated the *agora* (market place) which stretches southwards.

Market place

It is possible to clamber through the undergrowth into all that remains of the great meeting or market place. However the simplest route is to follow the road until the city walls are reached and then turn left down a gravelled track. This track then runs parallel with the perimeter of the agora in which can be seen one remaining pillar. It has been re-erected with its capital and the remains of the plaster, that would once have been painted in vibrant colours, can still be seen.

The excavation of the agora has never been completed and throughout its entire length only stumps of columns remain, with huge carved capitals lying abandoned all over the site in a haphazard fashion.

The agora would once have been a bustling market place and it is not too hard to imagine it furnished with fountains, shops and offices, and toga-clad figures going about their daily business.

At the southernmost end of the agora there is a **temple** dedicated to Zeus and thought to have been built early in the first century. Archaeologists discovered a plaque with a dedication to Livia who was Augustus's wife. The temple may have been built on the site of an earlier Hellenistic temple, but here again, excavations stopped and there is no visible conclusive evidence.

The harbour

Should the visitor be interested in finding the ancient harbour, it will be necessary to continue along the gravelled track and take the route towards the sea. Access by vehicle is not recommended close to the beach because the terrain is very sandy and it is easy to get stuck.

Snorkellers achieve great satisfaction from tracing the harbour outlines – it is not uncommon for artefacts to be found amongst the seaweed.

It must be emphasised that it is strictly illegal to take away any ancient artefact from the historical sites. All finds must be reported to the Ministry of Antiquities.

SITES AROUND SALAMIS

The Royal Tombs

From Salamis, there are, very close, two sites of historical interest. The nearest is that part of the expansive necropolis of Salamis which has been partly excavated to reveal what are referred to as the **Royal Tombs** and the **Cellarka**.

It has to be said that this is an area only of interest to those who are fascinated by ancient burial customs. There is little to be seen in the neglected museum and much of its contents have been dispersed elsewhere. At the time of writing there is work underway to refurnish the museum with appropriate artefacts.

The skeletons of the horses, slaughtered after performing their last task in transporting the body of their royal master to his burial place present grim testimony of the funeral ritual. Homer writes in 'The Iliad' of such sacrifices taking place, together with the slaughter of slaves or soldiers of the royal guard. At Salamis there has been scant evidence of human sacrifice but what has been found pertaining to the burial rite leads to the supposition that the customs that Homer wrote about spread with the Mycenaean people to Cyprus, and are not wholly myth.

Further evidence of these burial customs is to be found at **Enkomi ruins**. Of the tombs that have been excavated, several showed evidence of being used more than once, with burials taking place one on top of another. As the necropolis of

Salamis was in use for many hundreds of years this is not surprising and if the site is ever completely excavated it will reveal the different customs of the civilisations dwelling in the area during the centuries it was in use.

Each of the excavated tombs at the site has roughly the same constructional pattern with a sloping *dromos*, or driveway, leading down to the tomb entrance. It is at the bottom of the slope that the horse skeletons are to be seen where they have fallen in sacrifice. These are now to be found protected under perspex covers.

The burial chambers are hewn from solid limestone, and into the chamber the corpse would be placed with some of his personal possessions and food to sustain him on his journey to the next life. Apart from the skeletons of the horses there are no remaining artefacts of those buried in these tombs on show.

St Catherine's prison

The barrel-vaulted structure now known as St Catherine's prison also features a pair of horse skeletons in the dromos, and is a tomb that has had a multi-purpose function.

The original tomb structure is below ground level and was used successively from about the eighth century BC up until the fourth century AD when a vaulted chamber was built on top of it. The additional building was constructed from pieces of dressed masonry brought from different parts of the site. This is quite evident if the stonework is examined because few of the pieces fit together symmetrically.

According to legend, it was here that St Catherine was imprisoned after refusing to recant her new found faith of Christianity. She was tortured upon the wheel and eventually beheaded. She is commemorated by the 'Catherine wheel' firework.

Cellarka

The Cellarka are the smaller rock-cut tombs that were used for the burials of the lower orders of the city. They are adjacent to the Royal Tombs and their location is marked by a lone tree standing sentinel. There is a wire fence enclosing the area but this has long since been broken and access can be made at several points. The gate remains steadfastly padlocked.

Most interesting for the way in which the small tombs have been carved in a geometric pattern, each cluster of tomb chambers has a flight of stone steps leading down to it and the entrances were sealed with stone slabs. The tenure of the incumbents of the tombs would have depended on the rituals of the people of the time. In general the body would be placed in a terracotta vessel, such as a sarcophagus or a *pithos* and after nature had run the natural course of decay and decomposition, the remaining bones would have been removed allowing the burial chamber to be reused.

It is difficult to imagine the number of burials that would have taken place throughout the necropolis of Salamis during the centuries it was in use. Or again, to imagine the complex task of the sexton equivalent of those times, whose task it was to document and monitor the burials.

5 Karpas Peninsula

*T*he Karpas Peninsula or 'panhandle' as the British called the north-east part of Cyprus, is a land where time stands still. Miles and miles of sandy beaches with not a person in sight. Ancient towns, basilicas, ruins and tombs scatter the area waiting to be explored. To get a taste of Cyprus

twenty years ago, the traveller must visit the Karpas. These are not pretty, picture postcard villages like Bellapais, but rural traditional Cypriot villages where the animals live under the same roof as their owners. The land is agricultural and the majority of the villagers live off the land.

HISTORY

The peninsula has an important past. It was densely populated in Roman times, indeed Teucer, founder of Salamis, was said to have first landed on the Achaeans Beach near Yenierenköy. Trade links were strong between southern Turkey and Syria; the latter is only 70 miles (113km) away. With its plentiful stocks of timber and an abundant water supply, the Karpas made an excellent landfall for the seafarers of ancient times. It was one of the largest baronies under the Lusignans.

ROUTES ALONG THE PENINSULA

About 45 miles (75km) long it is roughly a three-hour drive from Girne to **Dipkarpaz**. The roads are good, but the journey is not to be rushed. A new road was constructed in 1999 bypassing many of the small villages. There are many places to stop at on the way, however they are not all easy to find and many tourists will take a guided tour to this area.

The quickest route is to leave Girne on the main Gazimağusa road. Take the left turn signposted Salamis and Mutluyaka. Drive past the church of St Barnabas and at the next junction turn left. You are now on the main road to the **Karpas**.

İskele

After roughly 5 miles (8km) the village of İskele (Trikomo) is signposted. 'İskele' means pier or jetty. The village is inhabited by many Turkish Cypriots who used to live in Larnaca before 1974, when the Turkish quarter of Larnaca was called İskele. The first steam engine on the island was set up to run cotton gins here in 1879. İskele was the home town of the Greek rebel leader George Grivas, born 23 May 1898. Son of a corn merchant, Grivas led the EOKA terrorists.

The village is famous for its pomegranates, which were a prominent crop of the lower Mesaoria area in the eighteenth century. Legend has it that Aphrodite first brought the fruit to Cyprus. In the centre of the village is a tiny church, the Dominican chapel of **Ayios Iakovos**. Queen Marie of Romania was so taken by it that she had a replica built on the Black Sea coast. The church is open during the day, although there are only a few ceramic plates as decoration to see on the inside. Take the left-hand fork in front of Ayios Iakovos and the domed twelfth century church of **Panayia Theotokos** is on the left.

Panayia Theotokos

This Byzantine building with its prominent frescoes is well worth a visit.

In the dome, worshipping angels surround Christ Pantocrator (ruler of the world). The letter IC and XC written in Byzantine style, in the two small circles, one each side of the figure, stand for the first and last letters in the name of Jesus Christ. Two archangels approach the preparation of the throne, which is flanked by the Virgin Mary and John the Baptist. The colours are still remarkably vibrant.

In the north aisle (a later addition

to the church) are Frankish-Byzantine frescoes of the fifteenth century. Most of the icons on display and those which make up the *iconostasis* (altar screen) are modern.

It is possible to pass behind the iconostasis into the belfry. The door represents the 'gates of heaven' and the Greek congregation do not pass this point (although visitors may do so). Set into the outside wall of the belfry is a carved marble stone, which came from the original iconostasis. It is interesting to see the reverse side of the iconostasis. The ropes and pulley system were to enable the Priest to take the icons out. On the various different saints' days the appropriate icon would be taken down and a procession of the clergy walked through the village carrying the icon. People would pass underneath it for a blessing.

Boğaz

Return to the roundabout and proceed straight across. Where this road joins the main road turn left for Boğaz. Boğaz is a fishing village with several restaurants, a couple of small shops and a petrol station. It is a good place to stop for a break and a drink. The small harbour was built and funded by the local fisherman and is exclusively for their use. In the mornings they stand on their boats selling the 'catch of the day'.

Simply follow the road northeast and enjoy the changing countryside. The people are very relaxed in the Karpas and this goes for the animals as well! Watch your speed, it is not uncommon to find two tractors stopped in the middle of

the road, their owners passing the time of day. The donkeys certainly have no respect for the Highway Code.

Church of Panayia Kanakaria

After passing **Kumyalı** (which the new road bypasses) follow the signs to **Ziyamet**. In the centre of the village turn right towards **Gelincik** and **Kaleburnu**. After about 2 miles (3.2km) the beautiful monastery church of Panayia Kanakaria is reached.

The building seen today incorporates some marble columns in the western narthex (entrance portico or vestibule) and Corinthian capitals from an earlier church. The apse was decorated with a famous sixth century mosaic of the Christ Child sitting on the lap of the Virgin Mary attended by two archangels and the apostles. It was believed that the coloured tesserae could cure skin diseases and therefore the mosaic suffered considerable damage. The remaining pieces were stolen by art thieves and some sold to a woman in Europe for one million dollars. She approached the Getty Museum in America who realised that these pieces should not be for sale on the open market. In 1989 the Greek authorities sued for the successful return to the island of the mosaic and the remains are now housed in a museum on the south side. The church is now kept locked at all times – the key can be obtained from the village *Muhtar*. It is possible to see the fresco of the Virgin Mary in the south portal and to admire the structure of this attractive building.

(cont'd on page 132)

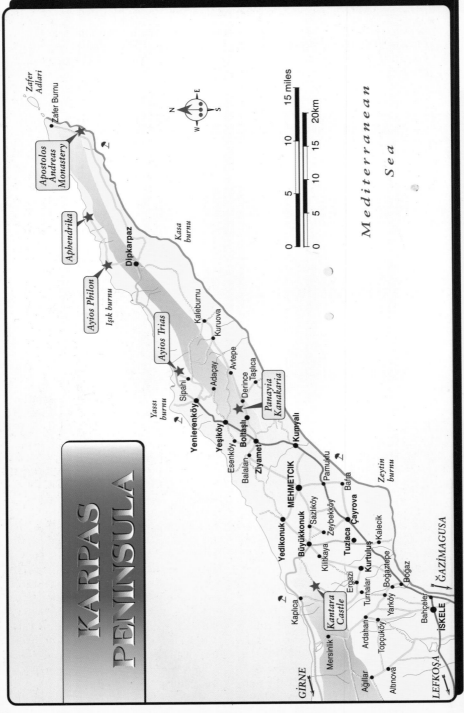

KARPAS PENINSULA

Mediterranean Sea

Zafer Adlari
Zafer Burnu

Apostolos Andreas Monastery

Aphendrika

Ayios Philon

Işık burnu

Dipkarpaz

Kasa burnu

Ayios Trias

Kaleburnu

Kuruova

Sipahi

Adaçay

Avtepe

Taşlıca

Yassı burnu

Yenierenköy

Yeşilköy

Derince

Panayia Kanakaria

Esenköy

Balalan

Boltaşlı

Ziyamet

Kumyalı

MEHMETÇIK

Pamuklu

Bafra

Zeytin burnu

Sazlıköy

Çayrova

Yedikonuk

Büyükkonuk

Zeybekköy

Kilitkaya

Tuzlaca

Kalecik

Kantara Castle

Ergazi

Kurtuluş

Boğaztepe

Boğaz

Kaplıca

Turnalar

Yarköy

Bahçeler

Mersinlik

Ardahan

Topçuköy

İSKELE

GİRNE

Ağıllar

Altınova

LEFKOŞA

GAZİMAGUSA

15 miles
20km
10
15
10
5
5
0
0

Above: Village children help sort the morning's catch at Yenierenköy

Left: Sandstone sculptures carved by wind and tide on the Karpas shores

Below: The village mosque at Dipkarpaz

Yeşilköy

Return to Ziyamet along the tarmac, where you turn right to resume the route. The next village is Yeşilköy which means 'green village'. The wonderful red soil is very fertile and among many other things, kolokas (a tuber similar to yam) is grown in this area.

Yenierenköy

Yenierenköy is a sizeable village with a petrol station. Most of the inhabitants today are refugees from **Erenköy** (Kokkina).

This is a village across the border in the far west of the island. In 1964 the village was badly attacked by Grivas and his EOKA terrorists. However the Turkish Cypriots of Erenköy resisted and Turkey intervened for the first time. The villagers and their supporters, who included Mr Rauf Denktaş (President of the TRNC), were cut off from the rest of the mainland. There was no way that they were prepared to let their village go, and in 1974 the village remained Turkish territory. Today Erenköy is an enclave under Turkish military control and can only be reached by sea. Once a year the inhabitants of Yenierenköy travel to Erenköy by boat for a celebration and com-miseration.

Before reaching the centre of Yenierenköy there is a signpost for Sipahi, turn right here. At the small square is the old **tobacco factory**. Go straight across the square and at the end of the road turn right. The road bears to the left, keep left and the road comes in to the village of Sipahi. Drive through Sipahi and as you leave

the village turn left, **Ayia Trias** is on the left opposite a house.

Tobacco industry

Tobacco was exported in quantity during the Middle Ages, most of it then growing in the Larnaca area. A factory operated near Limassol for a time in 1912 and used the local tobacco exclusively. Later the production area was moved to the Karpas, and the Department of Agriculture established a tobacco station for experimental purposes. The Tobacco Co-operative Society built the huge warehouse at Yenierenköy.

Traditionally it was the Turkish or Oriental variety which was grown. This type does not need such a rich soil. The tobacco seed was planted in box seed beds during January and February, transplanted to the fields in April and May. By July the leaves were ready for picking which continued until late October. It was a slow process. Once picked the tobacco leaf had to be cured. The old method was sun curing which took ten to twenty days. Now very little tobacco is grown.

Basilica of Ayia Trias

This sixth century basilica has some fascinating mosaics. At the west end of the building is the narthex or entrance leading into the church from an outer *atrium*. It has a central nave with an aisle on either side. An inscription in the front of the main apse records one Diacon Heraclios as a benefactor of the church. There is a **baptistery** to the south-east where the remains of the steps that led down to the font for immersion can be seen. Don't miss the delightful pair of **mosaic sandals,** which symbolise pilgrimage. The Bishop's residence was located to the west of the church.

THE COAST ROAD

After leaving Ayia Trias, turn right at the bottom of the road. You will now be following the coast. The **Theresa Hotel** is a small establishment offering refreshments and basic accommodation. To do the area justice two days are required and many people opt for a night in the Karpas, especially during the summer months. The Theresa has a main electricity supply whereas the accommodations further up must use generators. The drive is very pretty from here to Dipkarpaz.

Dipkarpaz

The villages in this area were built during Byzantine times. Dipkarpaz is home to the community of Greek Cypriots who wanted to stay in their own village after 1974. In the centre of the village is Andreas' coffee shop and the Greek priest sits outside the coffee shop drinking his 'Greek coffee'. Opposite, is his **church of Ayios Synesios.** Built in the twelfth century it was used under the Lusignans and Venetians as the cathedral of the Orthodox bishop of Gazimağusa. Many architectural and decorative

elements have been copied from St Sophia in Lefkoşa and St Nicholas in Gazimağusa. The church was enlarged in the eighteenth century. Dipkarpaz was one of the twelve Lusignan provinces of Cyprus and many wealthy people owned land and property here. In the mid-nineteenth century mulberry trees were grown here to support the silkworms. Residents of Dipkarpaz were noted for several centuries for the prevalence of blue eyes.

At Dipkarpaz there is a choice of routes. A right turn by the church heads out to the end of the peninsula via the south coast road, or bear left for the north coast and the ruins of Ayios Philon and Aphendrika.

Ayios Philon and Aphendrika

The road climbs the hill near the mosque, turn left at the top and then right. At the T-junction turn left and you will drive under an arch of a building, then left again. After passing the church turn right, the coast is now in front of you. The church of Ayios Philon is prominent on the shore. In the twelfth century this domed Byzantine church was erected on the site of an early fifth century Christian basilica, of which the foundations and mosaic floor patterns of the latter are to the south.

This is **Carpasia,** the ancient city that was of great importance during the Hellenistic period and Middle Ages. In 306BC Demetrius landed here in force following the death of Alexander the Great. It was not until eleven years later that Ptolemy expelled him.

Above: Boğaz fishermen weighing their catch

Left: One of the inhabitants of the Karpas Donkey Conservation Sanctuary

Carpasia became the seat of the bishop. Epiphanios, the Bishop of Salamis, ordained Philon as the first Bishop of Carpasia. The Roman harbour can be identified with two moles made of stone blocks, these were held together with metal clamps. The town was destroyed by the Saracens in 802AD and most of the remains have since been covered with sand.

Approximately 4.5 miles (7.2km) along the coast eastwards is **Aph-endrika**, known as one of the six major cities of Cyprus in the second century BC. Here are the remains of a necropolis with rock-cut tombs, a temple and the ancient harbour, which is now silted up.

The first ruin on the left is that of **Ayios Yeoryios** (St George). Originally a domed Byzantine structure built at the turn of the tenth century. It has a double apse with niches on either side.

Panayia Chrysiotissa, the largest

ruin, dates from the sixth century. It was destroyed during the Arab raids and the original wooden roofs were replaced with barrel vaulting at the end of the tenth century. It was again destroyed in medieval times and rebuilt in the sixteenth century.

Panayia Asomatos was also built in the sixth century and is similar in plan to Panayia Chrysiotissa. The Arabs also destroyed it but more features are remaining. The apsidal passages are easy to see, as is the vaulting over the south aisle.

Beyond Aphendrika the road turns into a rough track. During summer months it is passable by car with care but after rain it is full of deep water filled holes and should only be attempted on foot.

It is along here that the **'citadel'**, referred to in many guide books, can be found with much difficulty. It is certainly not worth the title of citadel. There are the remains of a settlement wherein the dwellings were created partially out of the rock with additional masonry placed to complete the walls and there are some entire rock-cut chambers with smoke holes in the roofs.

It is approximately a twenty-five to thirty minute walk from the churches of Aphendrika and the settlement nestles among a rocky outcrop on the right of the track. Almost directly opposite there are the remains of dilapidated shepherds' cottages. The shepherds now use what little is left of the dwellings to keep goats and sheep in at night. There is little else left

The mosaic floor in the Basilica of Ayios Trias at Sipahi

apart from some rock-cut tombs in the hillside. A climb to the top of the rocks, in search of some pointer to encourage belief in a great stronghold will disappoint. About a mile (1.6km) to the north from here is the harbour.

TO THE END OF THE PENINSULA

Back to Dipkarpaz take the alternative, southern, route to the end of the peninsula following the signs to **Zafer Burnu/Manastır**. The road soon follows the coast and there are many tracks, which lead down to the sea. It is a pleasant drive through cultivated land with many flocks of sheep and goats. The wild donkeys are to be found in this area, delightfully pretty, and with huge ears. Their numbers have been rising steadily over the last few years and they have had a special conservation area created for them.

An enormous stretch of sandy beach will soon come into view. This is one of the beaches used by the breeding turtles. Apostolos Andreas Monastery is only another 2 miles (3.2km) further.

Apostolos Andreas Monastery, the Lourdes of Cyprus

The monastery is dedicated to St Andrew, the miracle worker. The legend of St Andrew and this part of Cyprus goes back to apostolic times. On one of the saint's trips back to Jerusalem, he noticed that the one-eyed captain of the ship was in a panic as there was little fresh water left on board. They were just off the coast of Cyprus, where the monastery stands now.

St Andrew restored the sight of the captain there and then and ordered the sailors to go to the shore where they would find water. They found wells of drinking water. Thus the beginning of the monastery of St Andrew, the Lourdes of Cyprus.

Today there is little left of what is thought to have been the old chapel of the ancient buildings of the monastery. Situated next to the sea, there is a well in the corner that contains fresh water, which may be sampled outside the chapel. There are taps on the seaward side of the wall.

The main church is a fairly recent building and is looked after by the small community of Greeks who still live there. These old ladies will unlock the church for you and provide a candle for which they appreciate a small donation. The priest still travels up from Dipkarpaz to hold services at St Andreas.

Apostolos Andreas was not a monastery as the word generally implies. There used to be a monk who made sure that the pilgrims were given food and shelter, but it was just a parish church belonging to the community of Dipkarpaz. Thousands of pilgrims, including Moslems, would visit every year, especially on the feast days of 15th August and 30th November. The smaller buildings in the courtyard are where the pilgrims used to stay. Some would be deaf, dumb or blind and would all pray to the saint to be cured of their ailments. They would leave gold, silver and wax effigies, examples of which are in the church. The income left from the pilgrims made Apostolos Andreas a very wealthy monastery indeed.

After travelling this far it would be sad not to see the tip of the island. Follow the signs for Zafer Burnu and after two-thirds of a mile (1km) the road turns into a track. At the **Sea Bird Motel**, which is a conversion of the old British Customs and Excise offices there is a beautiful sandy beach. The beach has no facilities but refreshments can be purchased from Sea Bird where there are clean toilets and showers. Basic accommodation is also available.

It is the wonderful colours of the water, from light green to a deep blue that delight visitors at this beach. The bay alongside is normally full with fishing boats in the summer. The **Zafer Adaları** (Klidhes islands) lie beyond the cape. It is a truly wonderful view.

BEACHES IN THE KARPAS AREA

The beautiful, wild Karpas Peninsula has miles and miles of wonderful beaches. It is quite normal to share the seashore with the wild donkeys rather than other tourists. Go and explore, there is a bay to be found at the end of most roads.

Boğaz village, gateway to the Karpas has a small sandy bay which is managed by the Boğaz Hotel. There are several fish restaurants here so it is a good place to stop for refreshments. Watch the prices, they can be high.

Six miles (9.7km) from Boğaz is the village of Çayırova. Here a turning on the right leads through Bafra to **Bafra Bay**. A pleasant sandy beach with limited facilities.

Follow the newly built main road to Yenierenköy. Here you will find a petrol station and a small grocery shop selling the locally made wine. This is not very palatable. Passing the cheese factory on the left, the road drops down to the turning to **Malibu Beach**. There are some new holiday homes being built on the right hand side. The swimming is particularly good here, crystal clear water. Malibu Beach has a snack bar and some sun shades on the beach.

Dipkarpaz is a further 20 miles (32km) east. In the village, renowned for being the village where Greeks and Turks still live together, turn right and follow the signs for Apostolos Andreas Monastery. After travelling 3 miles (5km) you will come to **The Blue Sea Hotel**, one of the few basic hotels offering rudimentary facilities. Here is a small sandy bay.

Continuing along this road you pass the **Golden Beach Hotel**, which is only open in high season. It offers basic accommodation and chalets on stilts. The beach here is again sandy. It is most tranquil. Follow this road, it turns inland and the sea is lost behind shrub covered sand dunes. The land here is agricultural and you will see the flocks of sheep, goats and wild donkeys.

Stop your car on the roadside, turn off the engine and listen to the sound of goat bells, the hum of bees and the chatter of the wild birds. The tracks that lead off to the right here mostly go down to the sea. There are signposts down to the beach and there are cafés and picnic areas offering refreshments. This stretch of the coast is known as **Golden Sands** and it is 5 miles (8km) of wonderful solitude, even in high season. The turtles use this beach in the summer for nesting.

The Güzelyurt Area

6

*T*he western side of Northern Cyprus from Girne has the major archaeological sites, Vouni and Soli, and the town of Güzelyurt.

Vouni is fifth century BC, a hilltop palace with breathtaking views over the sea; **Soli**, a once Hellenistic city, taken over by the Romans when they had their turn at occupying the island. Here are some fine mosaic remains from the Roman era and, recently uncovered, there are some carved friezes from the Hellenistic period. In Güzelyurt there is the finest of the preserved churches of the Orthodox faith, the **church of St Mamas**, the patron

saint of tax avoiders and those who are suffering ear, nose and throat infections. **Pighades** is a Bronze Age site of great beauty, especially in spring.

TOURING THE AREA

The route from Girne to the west travels though mixed countryside; there is a lot of agriculture, including cereal crops, soft fruits and vegetables. Because the area is so varied it makes a very pleasant drive at all times of the year and there is always something being done in the fields, unlike crossing the eastern half of the Mesaoria plain, which is frequently dusty and boring.

Beaches

For approximately 12 miles (19km) westward the road follows the coast and there are many beaches for public use signposted off to the right. Of these the best are **Gulers Beach** at Kervansaray, **Sunset Beach, Mare Monte, Alsancak** and just before the road turns southwards away from the coast, **Güzelyalı Beach**, which has become very popular especially at the weekend.

Scenic diversion westwards

If a scenic drive is required turn right and follow the signs for **Kayalar** and **Sadrazamköy**, out towards the western tip of Koruçam cape. This road is narrow and follows a twisty route. It is however a beautiful drive if the idea is to get away from the madding crowd!

The main road after Güzelyalı beach next passes through the small village of **Geçitköy**. There is a large reservoir here, the dam of which is plainly visible to the left as the ascent is commenced up the winding road. This reservoir is one of the good bird watching sites and 'twitchers' from all over Europe visit it during the migratory seasons.

At the top of the hill a turning to the right is signposted **Çamlıbel** and **Güzelyurt**, this is the road to take unless Lefkoşa is the destination, in which case carry straight on. Çamlıbel is a small village (Myrtou pre-1974) which has a large army camp and a small enclave of ex-pats from various countries who live together in an area called **Anthos**.

The colour of the soil here changes to a rich red and is renowned for its fertility. Crops grow in abundance, evident on both sides of the road.

Tepebaşi is signposted to the left and **Sadrazamköy** and **Kayalar** to the right. After approximately 1 mile (1.6km) there is a petrol station on the right and a sign for **Akdeniz**. There is a beach here that is open to the public, however there is also a military area. Do not deviate from the beach road.

The route passes between plantations of young trees and large areas of limestone pavement upon which can be found dozens of tiny botanical specimens and wild herbs: sage, oregano and thyme scent the air.

After the village of **Kalkanlı** the road suddenly comes to the edge of the plateau and the panoramic vista opens across the western Mesaoria.

The great citrus orchards form a large dark green patch right in the middle and there are polythene hothouses growing vegetables. The road passes through the centre of the orchards and in the harvesting season there is a stall on the right selling oranges, lemons, melons, plums etc.

A Bronze Age copper centre

Just before a bridge across a dry riverbed, there is a turning to the right and the track leads down through the citrus to another turning on the right. Visitors are not encouraged, hence the lack of signposts, but it is here that the Bronze Age site of **Toumba tou Skoura** will be found.

This was an important centre for the export and working of the local copper, and dates from the same period as Enkomi. The copper mines were worked extensively in this area. Weapons for home use and export were made of bronze, an alloy of copper and tin. Fuel for the smelting process was readily available from the vast forests on the island.

Until iron replaced bronze as a hard metal, the mining of copper ore was one of the main industries of ancient times. The decline in the copper industry coincided with the decline of the Roman empire at the end of the fourth century. The burial customs were the same as Enkomi and comparable pottery artefacts were excavated. The excavations were carried out in the early 70s and since 1974 there has been no work on the site. Therefore, like the other remote and inaccessible areas of interest, nature has taken a strong hold on the visible remains. Many of the wonderful finds from here, including enormous *pithoi* are on display in the Güzelyurt museum.

Güzelyurt to Soli

The town of Güzelyurt (the name means 'beautiful country') is a mile or so further on. At the edge of the town on the lefthand side under some trees is a railway engine. One of the last pieces of rolling stock from the long deceased British-built railway. This is a 1920s American engine and is in a poor state of repair, but an interesting relic of the island's history.

Güzelyurt (Morphou) is a sprawling market town, which has grown due to the vast amount of agricultural produce it sells. It has a covered fruit and vegetable market and it would be difficult to find fresher produce. The **Natural History** and **Archaeological Museums** in what was once the Bishop's residence, and the church of St Mamas are the main reasons for stopping in the town on the way to, or returning from, Soli and Vouni.

The easiest way to negotiate the route through this town is to take the right turning at the first roundabout. The next junction is directly opposite the Archaeological Museum and here turn right to the next roundabout, right again and follow the signs for Lefke.

At the time of writing the road surface through this part of town is terrible. The *Belediye* (local council) will resurface the roads once all the drainage work, currently being carried out to improve the town sanitation facilities, has been completed.

There is some interesting light industry along this road including a factory that makes the wooden carcasses for chairs and sofas. There is also the Forestry Commission nursery where many different plants, shrubs and trees are grown. They are also available to buy and are naturally much cheaper than at a garden centre. Unfortunately many of these are unlabelled so it is essential to know your plants!

At the next junction turn right, the road is signposted **Gaziveren** and **Gemikonağı**.

Copper and golf

After **Yeşilyurt** the sea comes into view again on the right and then there is a sign to the **CMC (Cyprus Mines Corporation) Golf Club**. This is a 9-hole, 11-tee course, laid out as part of the entertainment facilities for mining corporation employees. The course is now run by ex-pat Brits and visitors are permitted to use the greens. However, it is advisable to contact the current captain manager Steve Brady (☎ 815 1861).

Green fees at present are £5.00 or Turkish Lira equivalent. Club days are Tuesday, Thursday and Sunday and no visitors are permitted to play on the last Tuesday of the month. The club welcomes players who have a golf handicap, as this is not a course for novices. Keen golfers coming with full equipment can leave their spiked shoes behind because these are not used on the course. Special shoes of a bowling green type can be hired from the clubhouse.

Modern copper mining

The Cyprus Mines Corporation, an American company, was responsible for reviving the copper mining industry. In 1911 C. Godfrey Gunther found a reference to the mines in Cyprus while reading a Latin manuscript in a New York library. The first mine opened by the CMC is believed to have been one of the ancient mines of Soli.

The sea from this point on starts to show discoloration in the water.

This is evidence of the seepage of chemicals from deep underground in the copper mines that are far out to the left. Three large fuel tanks, no longer in use are on the edge of the mining area and there is a bar on the shore called the **CMC Bar** run by the amiable Cemal (Jim). Behind the building is the rusting hulk of a tug that once saw better days escorting the fuel-laden vessels onto the unloading jetty.

The best fish and chips on the island are to be found at Cemal's and his bar is full of curios from the copper mines. The mining infrastructure is still remarkably intact despite being abandoned long ago. No serious copper mining has taken place here since the early 1970s.

The United Nations unification of Cyprus peace-keeping force has a large camp here and there are plenty of white UN vehicles with their blue beretted troops thronging the roads.

A few yards past the camps the turning left is to **Lefke**. This once prosperous mining town has now little to recommend it and is only worth a visit if the visitor has plenty of time to spare. Once the centre of mining in ancient times and a medieval barony, the town became predominantly Turkish after the Ottoman conquest and there are some interesting examples of Ottoman architecture to be seen here. These are now sadly in a dilapidated state and in need of urgent repair.

The town is renowned for the quality of its citrus produce, reputedly the finest on the island, benefiting from growing in an area that has a good water supply and excellent irrigation.

Above: Soli mosaic

Below: Statue of Artemis, the Goddess of Fertility in the Güzelyurt archaeological museum

THE ANCIENT CITY OF SOLI

From **Gemikonağı** the coast road runs close to the shore and heading westwards approximately one mile on the left is the **Soli Inn**, the road bears left slightly and the site of Soli comes into view, most prominent is the white roof that now covers the basilica floor. The turning on the left is quite well hidden and easy to miss.

The Antiquities Department have recently erected a hideous gantry roof (more in keeping with a cash and carry warehouse than with one of the finest ancient sites on the island) to cover the beautiful **mosaics** of the basilica floor. In so doing the aesthetic beauty of Soli has been completely destroyed. There is now very little natural lighting for the mosaics and it is difficult to make out the designs and pictures in the basilica floor. Perseverance will be rewarded with some wonderful bird, animal and floral designs.

The city of Soli, once one of the Ten City Kingdoms that made up the island at that time, was probably founded around the sixth century BC though it is possible there was once a much earlier settlement on this site. This rabidly pro-Greek city, was in continual conflict with the inhabitants of the palace of Vouni who were just as zealously pro-Persian. The Greeks were finally routed during the third century BC.

Roman remains

It is the Roman occupation of Soli that has left us with the remains that can be seen today. The **theatre** built into the hillside was relatively small and seated approximately 3,500. The rebuilt theatre of today, dating from the time of Swedish excavations which started during the 1930s and completed by the Department of Antiquities is overdone and somewhat tasteless, retaining none of its original qualities and charm. It cannot be compared with the theatre of Salamis, which is redolent with atmosphere.

The fifth century basilica was destroyed by the Arab raids of the seventh century and there are still the remains of mighty columns lying where they were originally toppled. The mosaics depict geese, duck, one glorious swan, dolphins, entwined vines and in the west atrium, a bear, a horse, bull and assorted fowl.

In the southern aisle there are fascinating geometric patterns.

During the twelfth century a much smaller church was built on top of the mosaics, covering them with brick and rubble to a depth of approximately 2ft (66cm). Certain sections of this smaller church floor have been removed exposing the mosaics beneath.

In time this second church crumbled and the stone work was removed during British occupation to strengthen the walls of the Suez Canal and continue the quay at Port Said.

The *agora* with a colonnaded street and *Nymphaeum* (an area decorated with statues of nymphs and ornamental fountains) are to be found across the field behind the custodian's office. Again this part of the site has been only partly excavated and there is little to see apart from a few carved capitals and the base of the marble fountain that was once dedicated to the Goddess Aphrodite.

The road to Vouni Palace

Returning to the road, turn left and continue in a westerly direction, passing through the village of **Yedidalga**. If driving with the car window open, the scent of fresh burning charcoal will soon assail your nostrils. The charcoal ovens are on the right and the industry of charcoal production is quite prolific.

The road winds upwards for just over a mile (2km) and at the top there is a yellow sign to the right for **Vouni Palace**. The road narrows and passes cottages with more charcoal ovens. (It is here that the author buys a large bag when visiting Vouni, at about £8.00 for a 55lb/ 25kg bag).

The ascent is very narrow and there are sheer drops to the right. Fortunately traffic is rare and encountering another car unlikely. It is however a good idea to make use of the horn, if for no other reason than announcing in advance that the custodian can expect a visitor. As the road reaches the top, the palace buildings are to be seen on the left. Continue driving round the perimeter of the palace until the parking area and custodians office are reached.

VOUNI PALACE

There is a good plan of the palace enabling the visitor to see the different stages of the buildings. Little remains now apart from the foundations, however the views from here are spectacular and walking from room to room it is not difficult to imagine the creativity and culture of the civilisation that built Vouni.

History of the palace

Constructed probably at the beginning of the fifth century BC, the Palace of Vouni was the creation of a pro-Persian Marionite king. Situated on the clifftop in an excellent strategic position, the inhabitants were able to look down at the pro-Greek city of Soli. As there was constant fighting between the two powers, it did not take long before the Greeks got the upper hand and took over the palace. In doing so they added more buildings and changed the entrance to the palace from the southern side, which was less impressive to an entrance up a broad flight of steps on the north-west corner.

What to see

The palace was destroyed by fire sometime after the Persians took control again and the site was abandoned round about 400BC. The dominating part of this palace is the **central courtyard**, which is reached up the entrance steps. It would originally have had a covered walkway on three sides, the broad stairs leading into the accommodation quarters for the hierarchy on the remaining side.

In the centre of the court there is one half of a stone stele which, with its counterpart, would have formed the windlass for drawing water from the central cistern. All water for this palace was collected in manmade underground chambers and there is a highly sophisticated sauna bath, and evidence of some very early water closets.

The complexity of the palace and the quantity of storerooms leads to the supposition that Vouni was built to stand the test of time. In fact it stood for approximately one hundred years, and in that time it had seen a change of rulers and no doubt much warfare.

To the south of the main building and at the highest point on the site will be found the bare outline of the **Temple of Athena**. The votive offerings found here, like all the other artefacts excavated from Vouni are in the Cyprus Museum situated in southern Nicosia, which cannot be visited.

On a spring day Vouni is a wonderful place for a picnic. The air is full of bird song and there is a carpet of wild flowers. A visit in summer will probably require a refreshing dip, the beaches at **Yedidalga** (seven waves) are clean and most have a café or bar situated close by.

GÜZELYURT

Returning to Güzelyurt, parking is available at the museum and it is a short walk into town. As stated earlier there is little to see in the centre except the large covered market. Entrance to the museums and **church of St Mamas** (see over leaf) is by ticket, which must be purchased from the custodian at the museum. The church is kept locked, the reason why is obvious once you enter it.

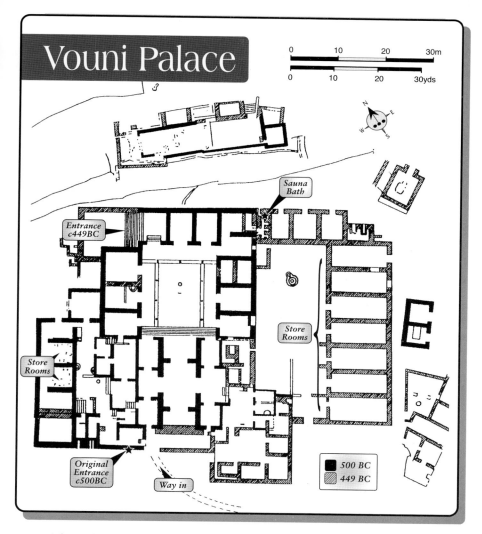

Vouni Palace

0   10   20   30m
0   10   20   30yds

Sauna Bath

Entrance c449BC

Store Rooms

Store Rooms

Original Entrance c500BC

Way in

■ 500 BC
▨ 449 BC

The **Gokkusağı restaurant,** which is opposite St Mamas, serves cold and hot drinks and excellent mixed kebab with salad.

Natural History & Archaeological Museums

The National History Museum on the ground floor of the one time Bishop's residence is full of a motley collection of specimens. From reptiles in murky jars of formaldehyde, to moth eaten stuffed birds and freaks of nature. Upstairs is the Archaeological Museum laid out chronologically in a series of rooms. All the artefacts are labelled and dated starting in Room I, with findings from the early Stone Age.

One of the rooms is dedicated almost exclusively to artefacts found at **Toumba tou Skoura** and in Room V can be seen some exquisite pieces of gold jewellery and a marble statue

(cont'd on page 148)

· CHURCH OF ST MAMAS ·

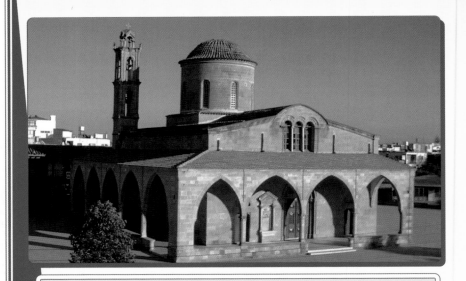

The late eighteenth century church of St Mamas is without question the most beautiful and the best maintained of the Orthodox churches that are preserved and open to the public as Icon Museums.

Inside the church

The church of St Mamas has long been an important place of pilgrimage and is only one of several churches on the island dedicated to this very popular saint. Larger and more spacious than many of the Orthodox churches, it is a mixture of Gothic and Byzantine architectural styles. There is an apse, three naves with pointed barrel vaults and the central nave is broader than the two at the sides. The dome of the church rises above the last two bays of the nave at the altar end and is pierced by six tall narrow windows.

The **tomb of the saint** is in the north wall and most of it is below ground level. The base of the tomb from inside the church can be accessed through a metal trap door in the church floor. This is not encouraged by the custodian.

St Mamas' tomb is pierced in the top and the hole is covered by a wooden lid. Lifting this lid will reveal the place where the pilgrims dip their fingers in the holy liquid, which oozes therefrom. This liquid has charged properties over the centuries according to writers who have documented it. Originally it flowed in abundance and was very sweet, changing then to the consistency of water (Holy Water of course) and now it smells most strongly of olive oil. No doubt the healing powers may be conveyed in whatever medium is deemed most fitting at the time, and I can personally attest to the powers of the present substance. An extremely painful earache was cured within twenty-four hours of applying the oil to the affected part.

The columns within the church, dividing the apse from the side aisles, are richly, albeit heavily, decorated. The carvings of foliar garlands, vine leaves and faces lack grace. However those columns that form part of the support for the iconostasis have been painted and the colours are warm and vibrant.

The *tympanum* over the marble sarcophagus of St Mamas is also painted and there is a painted panel in the archway depicting various scenes of martyrdom.

By far the finest exhibit in this church is the magnificent **chandelier** that hangs in the centre of the apse. It is flanked by a mixed assortment of no less elegant but much smaller chandeliers each of which is a work of art in its own right. The smaller ones cannot help but be eclipsed by the wondrous beauty of the hundreds of crystal droplets, each of which glows with all the colours of the rainbow in the reflected light from the surrounding bulbs. Reflected light because since the church was rewired in 1997 whenever the central chandelier is switched on it blows all the fuses. Consequently at the point of writing there is no chance of seeing the church illuminated to its full potential.

Legend of St Mamas

There is more than one legend concerning St Mamas, the one related here is the most charming. Mamas was a holy man and lived outside the town in a cave during the Roman/Byzantine period. Apparently he was supported totally by alms donated by the local people, in exchange for his prayers on their behalf.

When the Governor instituted a poll tax no-one was exempt, even those who lived in caves and had no money. Despite voluble protestations, Mamas was arrested and whilst being brought into the town, he saw a little lamb being attacked by a lion. Without hesitation, Mamas scooped that lamb up into his arms and jumped on the lion's back. He then rode into town to face the Governor. The latter was so impressed by the bravery and obvious holiness of Mamas (for who else but a holy man could have tamed the wild savagery of the lion?) that forthwith he was excluded from all tax demands. Hence the patron saint of tax avoiders.

(cont'd overleaf)

• CHURCH OF ST MAMAS •

(cont'd from previous page)

The church today

For all its being abandoned and unused for twenty-six years, this is one church that retains an air of sanctity and continuity. Maybe because it is so well kept and it is a credit to the custodians who look after it, or maybe because it is as the priest left it in 1974. His vestments still hang in a cupboard, the prayer books are open ready for a service and the wedding crowns and other paraphernalia are displayed in a glass-fronted case.

The main body of the church is still filled with the seats for the congregation, the microphone in place ready for the priest to commence his traditionally long homily. On the western outside wall of the church at the left corner is a delightfully naïve icon carved in the mellow sandstone, it is of St Mamas with the lamb in his arms astride a gently smiling lion. The monastic buildings built on two sides of the quadrangle have now been turned into shops and offices.

of the Goddess Artemis that was found by a diver off the shores at Salamis.

PIGHADES

The Bronze Age site of Pighades is reached by taking the Lefkoşa road from Güzelyurt and crossing the undulating plain. This road passes very close to the Atilla line, the border between north and south Cyprus, and tall sentry boxes can be seen to the right. After about 10 miles (16km) the road branches to the left for **Yilmazköy**, this is the route to take.

The road passes several army camps and cornfields roll away to left and right and after 6 to 7 miles (10-11km) on the left will be seen an avenue of fir trees interspersed with oleander bushes. This is the track to Pighades. It is unsignposted and can easily be missed. Negotiating the dry ditch takes care but it is

perfectly passable. The sanctuary of Pighades is enclosed by a wire fence and usually the gate is bolted. These are precautions to help keep out sheep and goats that would soon knock down the remaining walls of the ancient ruin.

At the centre of the complex of what were once rooms is the dominant structure of the rebuilt **altar**. It plainly shows the horns of the bull that was common to the sacrificial culture of the Bronze Age people. Similar altars have been found in Anatolia and Crete linking the worships of the people living in those areas.

The site was excavated in the early 1950s and the altar is very largely a reconstruction of dressed and decorated blocks. It is food for thought to wonder at the population that must once have worshipped their gods here. Somewhere in the surrounding land there are surely Bronze Age settlements waiting to be discovered.

This is a very beautiful site in spring and many orchids grow here along with the yellow leontice and wild gladioli (cornflag) struggling valiantly to make their presence seen among the tall splendour of the ubiquitous giant fennel.

Returning to the main road turn left and at the top of the slight hill on the left behind an army fence can be seen the ruined remains of the **Monastery of St Panteleimon**, one of the saints associated with the patronage of physicians. This eighteenth century church was abandoned in the 1950s having once been one of the residences of the Bishop of Girne. It is not accessible at the time of writing.

The road continues on towards Girne, and the Geticköy reservoir will be seen once again on the right.

There are alternative roads to be used to cross the Beşparmak mountains, see pages 90-97.

KORUÇAM

Maronite Christians

The Maronites first came to Cyprus from Syria, which then included Lebanon, sometime between the seventh and twelfth century. Established in the fifth century by followers of Ayios Maroni, a hermit of Syria, and forced to leave their homeland because of ill treatment by the Arabs, the Maronites settled in Lebanon. They are a Christian sect who show allegiance to the Pope but have their own liturgy.

The common language of the Maronites is Arabic, and the villagers of Koruçam have an Arabic dialect all their own. In 1224 there were some sixty Maronite villages, these had dropped to four by 1974. The dowry system here was 'bassackwards', meaning that the man built the bridal home.

Leave Güzelyurt on the main road heading back towards Girne. Look out for a sign to Tepebaşı, and once you have passed this sign slow down because it is easy to miss the sharp left turn for Koruçam and Sadrazamköy.

After turning off of the main road there is a military checkpoint, bear to the left and you will join the scenic road to Koruçam.

Koruçam (meaning 'grove of pines') is the main Maronite village on the island.

In the centre of the village is the enormous **church of St George** built in 1940 from funds raised by the villagers. On the other side of the road, in the garden of the convent, is the fifteenth century **convent church**. Although there is little to see inside, this church is lovingly cared for.

On the outskirts of the village, on the road to Sadralamkoy is the small barrel vaulted church of the **Panayia** (The Blessed Virgin Mary). This church is also looked after by the nuns and always has flowers on the altar. This is largely a farming community, and the young travel to the south in search of alternative employment. However the village comes alive at weekends when relatives cross the border to visit their families, and on Sundays it becomes clear why such a large church was built.

7 Lefkoşa (Nicosia)

*T*he divided capital city of Cyprus, Lefkoşa, lies in the Mesaoria, the central plain. To the north the rugged Kyrenia Mountains and to the south the Troodos Mountains make a spectacular backdrop. This inland position is unique, as all other major towns are on the coast and suffered terrible raids by the Arabs in the early Byzantine period. At this time it became far safer to be inland and for this reason Nicosia began to grow.

HISTORY

Nicosia was probably built on the site of the ancient city kingdom of Ledra. Lekfos, son of Ptolemy Soter, rebuilt the city in about 300BC. His name continues to be used by Cypriots in the local name for Nicosia, Lefkoşa. After the destruction of Constantia (Salamis), Nicosia grew to become an important centre of administration. In 1191 Richard the Lionheart sold Cyprus to Guy de Lusignan and from this time Nicosia remained the capital of Cyprus. The city flourished with the establishing of the French royal court. Splendid

Above: Street vendors in Lefkoşa selling pistachio nuts, chickpeas and honey

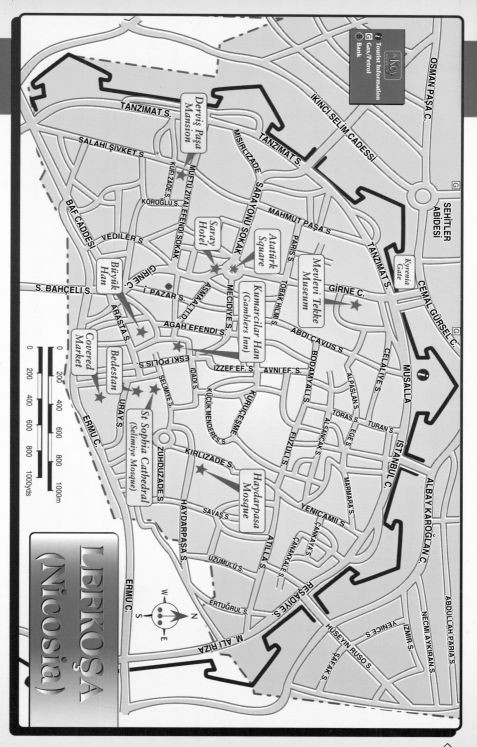

LEFKOŞA (Nicosia)

KEY
- *i* Tourist Information
- **G** Gas/Petrol
- **Bank**

OSMAN PAŞA C.

İKİNCİ SELİM CADESSİ

TANZIMAT S.

TANZIMAT S.

Derviş Paşa Mansion

SALAHI ŞIVKET S.

MISIRLIZADE

SARAYÖNÜ SOKAK

MAHMUT PAŞA S.

TANZIMAT S.

ŞEHİTLER ABİDESİ

Kyrenia Gate

BAF CADDESİ

VEDILER S.

MÜFTÜ ZIYAI EFENDI SOKAK

KÖROĞLU S.

KÜFİZADE S.

Saray Hotel

PARIS S.

Atatürk Square

Mevlevi Tekke Museum

TANZIMAT S.

GİRNE C.

Büyük Han

GİRNE C.

S. BAHÇELİ S.

İ. PAZAR S.

ASMALTI S.

MECİDIYE S.

Kumarcilar Han (Gambler's Inn)

TOBAK HİLMİ S.

ABDI ÇAVUS S.

CELALIYE S.

MUSALLA

İSTANBUL C.

CEMAL GÜRSEL C.

ARASTA S.

AGAH EFENDI S.

Covered Market

Bedestan

ESKİ POLİS S.

İZZET EF. S.

AVNİ EF. S.

İDADI S.

BODAMYALI S.

ALPASLAN S.

TORAS S.

EGE S.

TURAN S.

FUZULI S.

ALBAY KAROĞLAN C.

ERMU C.

URAY S.

SELİMİYE S.

KÜÇÜK MENDERES S.

KURUÇEŞME

ALSANCAK S.

MARMARA S.

St Sophia Cathedral (Selimiye Mosque)

ZUHDUZADE S.

KIRLIZADE S.

Haydarpaşa Mosque

YENİCAMII S.

HAYDARPAŞA S.

SAVAŞ S.

ÜZÜMLÜ S.

ATİLLA S.

ÇANAKALE S.

ÇANKAYA S.

RESADIYE S.

ERTUĞRUL S.

ERMU C.

M. ALİ RIZA

HÜSEYİN RUSO S.

YENİCE S.

ŞAFAK S.

İZMİR S.

NECMİ AYKIRAN C.

ABDULLAH PARIA S.

0 200 400 600 800 1000m

0 200 400 600 800 1000yds

W N E S

· Shopping in Lefkoşa ·

Lefkoşa is a very interesting city. You must take yourself down the winding 'rabbit warren' streets to see the heart of this old-fashioned capital. As in past times everything closes at 12.30pm for siesta, so morning is the best time to visit. Saturdays is half-day closing. As with all capital cities keep your belongings safe and do not carry large amounts of cash.

The **covered market**, next to the Selimye Mosque, is well worth a visit. Although small you will find an amazing array of goods. Now is the time to buy Turkish Delight (*lokum*). Every flavour that you can possibly think of is available. Be sure to 'try before you buy'. Look out for the old whisky bottles re-filled with locally pressed olive oil.

Take a look in the small **copper shop**. There are some lovely unusual pieces including copper *cezves*. A cezve is the traditional pot used to make Turkish coffee. You will also find a stall selling **handmade lace**.

After leaving the market, walk the very short distance to the mosque and turn left. About 400 yards (366m) along this road on the left is the **Helva kiosk**. *Helva* is a sweetmeat made of crushed sesame seeds and

palaces and churches were built alongside grand houses.

Despite the inland position, the Mamelukes from Egypt invaded in 1426. The beautiful city was plundered and many of the magnificent buildings were burnt to the ground.

After the Venetians gained control of Cyprus in 1489, Nicosia was radically changed. They wanted the city to be fortified by a circular earthwork with eleven bastions, three gates and a ditch. The city circumference was reduced from 7 to 3 miles (11·5km) and the building of these defences was put into operation. With a watchful eye on the Ottomans, the Venetians commissioned their military engineer Julius Savorgnano.

In 1567 the massive wall was built around the perimeter of the reduced city. It can still be seen today, with its eleven bastions clad in stone. The ditch never materialised; instead a dry moat encircled the walls. Most of the palaces and churches remaining at that point were destroyed in order to clear the line of fire for the artillery. The greatest loss was

the royal castle and the monastery of San Domenico, whose church housed the tombs of the Lusignan dynasty. The work progressed very slowly and was not finished when the Ottomans arrived.

Despite these preparations, Nicosia fell to the Ottoman forces under Lala Mustapha Paşa after a siege lasting only six weeks. Canon fire was used against the great Venetian walls. The defence was in disarray with no Commander-in-Chief. Nicholas Dandolo, the acting commander, was a very incompetent man and relied upon Venice sending an army. The troops who were there were untrained and unfed.

Lala Mustapha moved his men right underneath the walls. Gunners could have halted this move but shot was rationed. When Mustapha found out from his spies that no reinforcements were coming he sent for extra men from his base camp and made his final assault. There was an orgy of slaughter and it is recorded that 20,000 people were massacred.

sugar. Delicious either on its own or spread on fresh bread, the Cypriot way. The Helva is made on the premises daily. It can be kept fresh by storing in a refrigerator.

Continue walking straight ahead and you will come into a small street full of rolls and rolls of material for sale. There are many tailors who will make a suit in a matter of days and the price is reasonable too.

As you are strolling around you will see the **'barrow boys'**, or barrow *men* to be more precise. They shout out what they are selling and the price per kilo. Some sell traditional Turkish snacks like *tulumba* (sweet pastry) and *simit* (bread rings).

A **backgammon** board is sure to be a wonderful reminder of Cyprus. It is a national pastime and you will see men playing it everywhere, especially in the coffee shops. You will find boards of all different sizes and colours on offer, and maybe even learn a few moves from a Cypriot!

Cash

As Lefkoşa does not have the tourist trade that Girne has, there are not many exchange bureaux to be found. There are however plenty of banks. The **İş Bankasi** at the top of the high street (Girne Caddesi) has a cash point machine, be prepared for long queues.

The capital city went rapidly into decline and never regained its former prosperity. When the British came in 1878 the city was in a terrible state. The fine buildings were in ruins and the population only totalled 11,500. The British installed utilities, built roads and undertook to establish Nicosia as a modern city.

With a population of 38,500, the Nicosia/Lefkoşa of today is most interesting. Approximately 37 per cent of this divided capital city lies in the northern sector. There are two distinct areas, the old and the new. Inside the old walled city, sandstone buildings with wooden balconies line the narrow, winding streets. In the quieter areas time seems to have stood still. Driving is not recommended. There is a complicated one way system, which is most difficult to get out of once in.

TOURING THE CITY

Girne Gate

The best way into the old city is through **Girne Gate**. Situated at the bottom of the main street, this was part of the Venetian walls until 1931 when the British built roads on either side to allow for traffic. There is a marble plaque inscribed in Latin giving 1562 as the date of construction. The Arabic script on the outside of the gate reads,

"O Mohammed, give these tidings to the faithful: victory is from God, and triumph is near. O opener of doors, open for us the best of all doors."

Mevlevi Tekke Museum

Just past Girne Gate on the left is the Mevlevi Tekke. A *Tekke* is a religious lodging house. This was

Above: Inside the Buyuk Han. The central domed building is a mosque with ablution facilities beneath

Left: Arabic inscription over the entrance gate to the Mevlevi Tekke

home to the Mevlevi Order founded by the poet Jelal-ed-din Roumi Mevlana in the thirteenth century. The Muslim monks were commonly known as The Whirling Derviş due to the dance that they performed.

The music was composed by Jelal and played mainly on a reed flute and drum. Wearing their white cassock-style robes the Derviş whirled themselves into ecstasy. They would dance with one palm held up to heaven and the other downward to earth symbolising man as a bridge between earth and heaven. One Derviş would stand in the centre of the dance floor representing the sun and the planets. Atatürk banned the order in 1925, and the last Derviş in Cyprus died in 1954. There is a long room containing the tombs of the various Derviş. This seventeenth century building is now used as a museum.

Above: Locals and tourists sitting together playing Backgammon

Below: The Bedestan converted by the Ottomans into the covered market and now undergoing restoration

Atatürk Square

A five-minute walk from Girne Gate is the main square of Lefkoşa. The grey granite column was erected by the Venetians, with the lion of St Mark on top, as a symbol of their rule. This was quickly torn down during the Ottoman conquest. The British re-erected it early this century, replacing the lost lion with a copper globe. Its base is decorated with the Venetian coat of arms.

Some superb British colonial-style buildings can be seen to the north of the square. This was formerly the site of the Venetian governor's palace.

Not to be missed is a visit to the **Saray Hotel**. Take the lift to the eighth floor. From here is the most amazing and interesting view over this divided capital. A lift charge is applicable but this ticket may be exchanged for a drink at the bar.

St Sophia Cathedral
(Selimiye Mosque)

St Sophia is one of the most impressive Gothic works of architecture in Cyprus. The name St Sophia is taken from the earlier Byzantine building that was on the same site. 'Sophia' means divine wisdom.

History of the cathedral

The foundation stone was laid in 1209 during the incumbency of the Latin Archbishop Thierry. While visiting Cyprus in 1248 on his way to the Crusades, King Louis IX of France supplied many engineers and artisans. It was a slow process. Indeed it was not until 1326 that the cathedral was consecrated, although some work was still unfinished.

It was in St Sophia that the Lusignans were crowned as kings of Cyprus. It suffered damage by the Genoese in 1373 and again by the Mamelukes in 1426. The Lusignans carried out some repairs, but once the Venetians came, the treasure was taken. The cathedral was to suffer again during the earthquakes of 1491 and 1547.

Francesco Contarini, the Bishop of Paphos, gave the last Catholic mass on September 9th 1570. As soon as a city is taken in *jihad*, or holy war, a mosque must be created to symbolise the power of the Muslim faith. The easiest and quickest method therefore is to take an existing building and convert it into a mosque. This was to be the fate of St Sophia. A mosque is simply a shelter to worship. Swiftly converted to a mosque by the Ottomans, all Christian features were stripped with the exception of some tombstones. The beautiful stained glass windows were removed and the interior decorations and statues plundered. Lastly the two huge minarets were added to call the faithful to prayer.

Entering the cathedral

The edifice begins with a grand entrance, above which is a magnificent traceried window, flanked by two towers, which were never completed and since converted into minarets. The porch itself is massive, built in three sections, matching the three entrances to the nave and the aisles. The decoration here is most impressive. In front of the porch is where the men carry out their ablutions before entering the mosque to pray. Women must clean themselves before arriving. In line with the Muslim faith, visitors must remove their footwear before proceeding inside the building.

Two rows of six massive columns divide the inside. These are linked in the apse by four granite columns with Byzantine capitals. This form of architecture was popular in Cyprus as a precaution against earthquakes. Along either side of the aisles is the bare, raised gallery, accessed by staircases to the right and left of the aisles.

The chapel

The chapel in the north transept was consecrated to St Nicholas. The staircase here leads to the Moslem women's gallery. In the southern transept was the chapel of the Virgin Mary. A *mihrab* has been erected here: this is in the form of a niche in the wall, painted with Arabic inscriptions, it is known as the gateway to Mecca, its orientation is directed to Mecca. Near the mihrab is the *mimbar*, which is a high pulpit and it recalls the seat of the Prophet. It is said that if you make a wish whilst passing through the gap underneath the seat it will come true. The next chapel was dedicated to St Thomas Aquinas and there are some fine gravestones here from the Middle Ages.

In 1954 the mosque was renamed Selimye Mosque in honour of Sultan Selim II in whose reign the Turks captured the island.

The Bedestan

On the south side of St Sophia is the former Greek Orthodox cathedral, which the Ottomans converted to a covered market or *Bedestan*. Originally built by the Byzantines in the twelfth century, the nave and north aisle date from the fifteenth century

giving the building its Gothic elements. The three portals inserted into the north wall are finely carved with some wonderfully preserved **gargoyles**. The middle door has a carved marble relief of the death of the Virgin Mary.

Büyük Han

Büyük Han or Great Inn was built in 1572 by the first Ottoman Governor of Cyprus. There are numerous Hans similar to this in the Anatolian region of Turkey. These inns or caravanserais were to offer the traveller safe accommodation and at the same time a place to trade, sell and store goods.

The rooms on the upper floor were for lodging with fitted carpets and fireplaces (the small chimneys are easy to spot). On the ground floor would be shops, storage rooms and offices. The stables were located outside the inn. In the middle of the courtyard is a small domed mosque. At the time of writing there is extensive renovation work being carried out.

Derviş Paşa Konak

The house dates from the nineteenth century and is named after its former owner. Derviş Paşa was the publisher of the first Turkish newspaper in Cyprus *Zaman*, or 'Time'. The mansion was brought back to its former glory in 1988 and opened as a museum.

The ground floor was used as a store and for servants, the upper floor for the family with women's quarters and a reception hall or *selamlık*. This was the most important room in the whole of the house where guests were received.

Fact File ↑

ACCOMMODATION

Northern Cyprus offers a wide range of accommodation from private villas and self-catering holiday villages to resort hotels. There is a star grading system. These stars are awarded locally and should not be confused with international standards.

The majority of tourists come on a package holiday which is much the best idea. There are only 8,500 tourist beds available. During August, September and October it is difficult to find space anywhere. The different accommodations are described in some detail in the brochures of tour operators that specialise in Northern Cyprus. Full details of the tour operators can be obtained from:

Representatives of the TRNC, 29, Bedford Square, London WC1B 3EG, UK, ☎ 0207 631 1930, Fax 0207 631 1873.

Ahmet Erdengiz, 1667, K Street, Suite 690, Washington, USA, ☎ 202 887 6198, Fax 202 467 0685, e-mail kktc@erols.com.

Aytuğ Plümer, 821 United Nation Plaza, 6th Floor, New York, NY 10017, USA, ☎ 212 687 2350, Fax 212 949 6872, e-mail TRNCNY@aol.com.

The star rating is given locally and SHOULD NOT be confused with the internationally recognised system.

Girne Area

The Dome Hotel ****
PO Box 6
Girne
Mersin 10. Turkey
☎ (392) 815 2453,
Fax (392) 815 2772
Best position in Girne,
refurbished (1998/1999).

Dedeman Olive Tree ****
Çatalköy
Mersin 10. Turkey
☎ (392) 824 4200,
Fax (392) 824 4209
Collection of hotel rooms and villas in beautiful grounds, 6 miles (9.7km) from Girne.

Bellapais Gardens ****
Crusader Road
Bellapais
Mersin 10. Turkey
☎ (392) 815 6066,
Fax (392) 815 7667
In beautiful Bellapais, very quiet, not suitable for small children.

The Hideaway Club ****
PO Box 617
Girne
Mersin 10. Turkey
☎ (392) 822 2620,
Fax (392) 822 3046
Collection of bungalows and suites, wonderful hospitality.

The British Hotel ***
Eftal Akça Sokak
Yat Limanı, Girne
Mersin 10. Turkey
☎ (392) 815 2240,
Fax (392) 815 2742
Comfortable hotel in Girne Harbour.

Mare Monte Hotel ***
PO Box 222. Alsancak
Girne, Mersin 10. Turkey
☎ (392) 821 8310,
Fax (392) 821 8887
Beautiful beachfront location, choice of basic hotel and bungalow accommodation, 7 miles (11km) from Girne.

Deniz Kızı Royal ****
PO Box 230, Alsancak
Girne, Mersin 10. Turkey
☎ (392) 821 2676,
Fax (392) 821 8433
On one of the most popular
beaches in the area, 5 miles
(8km) from Girne.

LA Hotel ****
Maraşal Fevzi Çakmak Cad.
Lapta, Girne
Mersin 10. Turkey
☎ (392) 821 8981,
Fax (392) 821 8992
Modern complex with sandy
beach, 10 miles (16km) from
Girne.

Gazimağusa Area
The Palm Beach ****
Deve Limanı, Gazimağusa
Mersin 10. Turkey
☎ (392) 366 2000,
Fax (392) 366 2002
Beachfront hotel outside of the
old walled city in Gazimağusa.

Mimoza Hotel ***
Salamis Yolu, Gazimağusa
Mersin 10. Turkey
☎ (392) 378 8119,
Fax (392) 378 9077
Basic beachfront hotel, very
popular with locals, 11 miles
(17.7km) from Gazimağusa.

CAR HIRE

Driving is on the left with the majority of hire cars being right-
hand drive. This makes things easy! It is advisable when travelling
in high season to pre-book the vehicle from the tour operator as
availability of good quality vehicles is low.

There is a multitude of organisations but care must be taken.
There are many car hire companies, some better than others.
Check with the hirer what their breakdown procedure is and
always pay for collision damage waiver.

It is safer and easier to book with your tour representative as,
unlike other destinations, a large commission is not charged to
the client. Make sure that the price quoted covers collision damage waiver and local value added tax which is 10 per cent. **The
wearing of seatbelts in the front of the vehicle is law**. Alcohol
should be avoided when driving.

Always make sure you have sufficient fuel as petrol stations can
be few and far between especially the ones selling unleaded fuel.
Report any accident directly to the nearest Police Station. Look
out for yellow-and-white or black-and-white painted kerbs. This
means no parking. The speed restrictions are shown in kilometres. Watch your speed, as the police have roadside checks.

Car hire companies

KTS
PO Box 358
Girne
Mersin 10. Turkey
☎ (392) 815 7555,
Fax (392) 815 7730
e-mail kts@cypronet.net

Pacific Rent A Car
23 Ecevit Sokak
Girne
Mersin 10. Turkey
☎ (392) 815 2508,
Fax (392) 815 5570

Fact File

Arizona Ltd
B11, Eçevit Sokak
Girne
Mersin 10. Turkey
☎ (392) 815 1355,
Fax (392) 815 1356

British Car Rentals
Eftal Akça Sokak
Yat Limanı, Girne
Mersin 10. Turkey
☎ (392) 815 5731,
Fax (392) 815 2742

CLIMATE

Contrary to popular belief, it can be cold in Northern Cyprus. Although there is no frost or ice and only snow on the mountain-tops in very rare conditions, a visitor arriving during December through to April will need to pack clothing for all weathers.

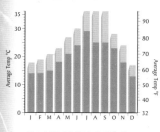

A Cypriot will tell you that summer does not begin until May 15th. The daytime temperatures can be pleasant but as soon as the sun sinks the cold evening air bites. The wettest months are January and February. July and August are for dedicated sun worshipers as the mid-day temperature can soar well over 100°F (35°C).

CURRENCY

The local money is the ever-escalating Turkish Lira. Everyone becomes a millionaire overnight. Sterling is readily accepted. US dollars are readily accepted in larger stores. Sterling is the best form of currency to bring. If you feel uncomfortable carrying large amounts of cash then sterling or dollar travellers cheques are easily exchanged in banks, exchange bureaux and hotels. Do not bring Turkish Lira as the exchange rates are much better in Northern Cyprus.

There are several banks in the main towns with cashpoint machines. The card must have the international visa sign. Credit cards are not widely accepted and carry a surcharge between 2-8 per cent. Eurocheques are also given the cold shoulder. Hardly any establishments will cash a personal cheque.

ELECTRICITY

Throughout Northern Cyprus, voltage is 220/240 volts AC and sockets are usually of the 3-pin British type. Most anti-mosquito machines are fitted with the continental 2-pin type of plug so an adapter will be required.

Men should take wet razors as very few accommodations have a shaver point. Power cuts can occur at any time, however they are becoming less frequent. The larger hotels and holiday villages have their own generators. A torch may also be useful as there is little or no street lighting in the villages and along the minor roads.

HEALTH

British medications for holiday ailments are stocked by the main chemists. The prices can range from well below UK price to more than triple! There are many English-speaking doctors who have their own private clinics. Medical treatment is not cheap so holiday insurance is essential.

Most upset stomachs are caused by a mixture of too much sun, alcohol and a change in the diet. Imodium quickly disposes of the problem. Some people have a nasty reaction to mosquito and sand fly bites. Try rubbing anti-histamine cream on the affected part.

A good sun block lotion should be used and direct sunlight on the head should be avoided. Take plenty of non-alcoholic drinks throughout the day.

Snake bites are rare but should the worst happen, cover the bite with a cloth. Apply a tourniquet above the bite if it is on a limb but not so tight as to cut the blood supply off. Seek medical attention immediately.

MAPS

A selection of maps are produced by the tourist board. You can collect these free from the tourist information offices or from your travel rep. Maps purchased outside Northern Cyprus normally have Greek place names which are of no use when travelling around the Turkish North. The accuracy of roads is also doubtful due to the Military restrictions in Northern Cyprus.

MUSEUMS AND HISTORICAL SITES

During summer the opening times are 9am-1pm and 2-4.45pm.

Winter hours vary. The smaller indoor museums are open from 9am-2pm and the larger outdoor sites from 9am-5pm. The curators take into account how long a visit lasts; for St Hilarion it takes roughly 2 hours to explore the site, so last admittance is 3pm.

NEWSPAPERS AND MAGAZINES

English-language publications are a rarity in Northern Cyprus. Do not leave your newspapers on the plane as they make a great gift for the travel representative or accommodation owner. *Cyprus Today* is a weekly newspaper and is most useful for visitors. It contains lots of local news and advertisements of the various restaurants and events taking place. *The Daily News* is printed in English and has world news.

NUDISM

Topless sunbathing on the beach is not frowned on but the local male population do tend to stare. It is best to check with the individual hotel reception for their policy on this matter as some accommodations are family based. Nudism is not permitted in Northern Cyprus.

PACKING

A visit to Northern Cyprus during the summer requires few clothes. The standard allowance permitted by the airlines is 62lbs (28kg) plus a small piece of hand luggage. There is no formal dress code in the restaurants for dinner. A pair of lightweight trousers and short sleeve shirt for men, skirt and blouse for women. A jacket or a cardigan may be useful for the evenings. Toiletries and a small first aid kit should be brought. Camera film is cheaper in Cyprus.

Do not be surprised if there are no plugs in the bathroom; take an adaptable rubber plug.

PASSPORTS

All visitors to Northern Cyprus must have a full 10 year passport.

POSTAGE

Stamps may be purchased from post offices and some hotel receptions. Mail sent to Europe should arrive in 7 days. Do not use the small yellow post boxes in the villages as collection from these is rare! It is best to leave your mail on reception or at the post offices.

PHOTOGRAPHY

There are many breath taking views and stunning scenery in Northern Cyprus. As in most countries the photographing of military sites is forbidden. There are many red signs, written in four different languages placed where the military areas are. Do not attempt to photograph anywhere near these areas.

TURKISH/GREEK PLACE NAMES

Many tourists returning to Cyprus remember the Greek place names. Nicosia/Lefkoşa, Kyrenia/Girne and Famagusta/Gazimağusa are used interchangeably by locals and visitors alike, but all other places are known by their Turkish names, and so the following list should aid the traveller.

Turkish to Greek

Ağirdağ	Aghirda	İskele	Trikomon
Akdeniz	Agia Irini	Ilgaz	Ftericha
Alevkaya	Halevga	Kalkanlı	Kalon Chorion
Alsancak	Karavas	Karaağaç	Charkeia
Arapköy	Klepini	Kaplıca	Davlos
Aslanköy	Angastina	Karakum	Karakoumi
Avtepe	Ayios Symeon	Karaman	Karmi
Aydınköy	Prastion	Karaoğlanoğlu	Ayios Georgios
Bafra	Vokolida	Karpaşa	Karpaseia
Beşparmak	Trapeza	Karpaz	
Beylerbeyi	Bellapais	Yardımadası	Karpasia
Boğaz	Bogazi	Kayalar	Orga
Büyükkonak	Komi	Koruçam	Kormakitis
Çamlıbel	Myrtou	Koruçam Burnu	Cape Kormakiti
Çatalköy	Agios Epiktitos	Kumlayı	Koma tou
Çayırova	Agios		Gialou
	Theodoros	Lapta	Lapithos
Dipkarpaz	Rizokarpaso	Lefke	Lefke
Doğanköy	Thermeia	Lefkoşa	Lefkosia/Nicosia
Dörtyol	Prastion	Malatya	Palaiosofos
Edremit	Trimithi	Maraş	Varosha
Esentepe	Agios Amvrosios	Mersinlik	Flamoudi
Erenköy	Kokkina	Mesarya	Mesaoria
Gaziveren	Kazivera	Mevlevi	Kyra
Geçitkale	Lefkoniko	Ozanköy	Kazafani
Geçitköy	Panagra	Pamuklu	Tavrou
Gemikonağı	Karavostasi	Sadrazamköy	Livera
Girne	Kyrenia	Tepebaşı	Diorios
Güneşköy	Nikitas	Yeşilyurt	Pentageia
Güzelyurt	Morfou	Yedidalga	Potamos tou
Gazimağusa			Kambou
Körfezi	Famagusta Bay	Yenierenköy	Agialousa
Gazimağusa	Famagusta	Zeytinlik	Templos

Greek to Turkish

Aghirda	Ağirdag	Davlos	Kaplıca
Agia Irini	Akdeniz	Diorios	Tepebaşı
Agios Amvrosios	Esentepe	Famagusta	Gazimağusa
Agios Epiktitos	Çatalköy	Famagusta Bay	Gazimağusa
Agios Theodoros	Çayırova		Körfezi
Agialousa	Yenierenköy	Flamoudi	Mersinlik
Angastina	Aslanköy	Ftericha	Ilgaz
Ayios Georgios	Karaoğlanoğlu	Halevga	Alevkaya
Ayios Symeon	Avtepe	Kalon Chorion	Kalkanlı
Bellapais	Beylerbeyi	Karakoumi	Karakum
Bogazi	Boğaz	Karavas	Alsancak
Cape Kormakiti	Koruçam Burnu	Karavostasi	Gemikonağı
Charkeia	Karaağaç	Karmi	Karaman

Karpaseia	Karpaşa	Myrtou	Çamlıbel
Karpasia	Karpaz	Nikitas	Güneşköy
	Yardımadası	Orga	Kayalar
Kazafani	Ozanköy	Palaiosofos	Malatya
Kazivera	Gaziveren	Panagra	Geçitköy
Klepini	Arapköy	Pentageia	Yeşilyurt
Kokkina	Erenköy	Potamos tou	
Koma tou Gialou	Kumlayı	Kambou	Yedidalga
Komi	Büyükkonak	Prastion	Aydınköy
Kormakitis	Koruçam	Prastion	Dörtyol
Kyra	Mevlevi	Rizokarpaso	Dipkarpaz
Kyrenia	Girne	Tavrou	Pamuklu
Lapithos	Lapta	Templos	Zeytinlik
Lefke	Lefke	Thermeia	Doğanköy
Lefkoniko	Geçitkale	Trapeza	Beşparmak
Lefkosia/Nicosia	Lefkoşa	Trikomon	İskele
Livera	Sadrazamköy	Trimithi	Edremit
Mesaoria	Mesarya	Varosha	Maraş
Morfou	Güzelyurt	Vokolida	Bafra

PUBLIC HOLIDAYS AND FESTIVALS

The religious holidays of Islam are observed, these are calculated by the phases of the moon. Ask your travel agent for advice or check the current Muslim calendar dates before you travel.

Ramadan lasts for 30 days. It is the month of fasting followed by 3 days of celebration. Many Turks take a holiday at the end of Ramadan, making it a busy time on the island. **Kurban Bayram** (Feast of the Sacrifice) lasts for four days. The head of each household buys a lamb. A sacrifice is made of the lamb and it is shared with the whole family and with the poor. Again this is a popular period for a holiday. Northern Cyprus has nine additional public holidays:

1st January	**New Years Day**
23rd April	**Children's Day**
1st May	**Labour Day**
19th May	**Youth and Sports Day**
20th July	**Peace and Freedom Day** (the anniversary of the Turkish troops landing)
1st August	**Communal Resistance Day** (the anniversary of the Ottoman conquest of Gazimağusa in 1571)
30th August	**Victory Day**
29th October	**Turkish National Day**
15th November	**Independence Day** (proclamation of the TRNC)

PUBLIC TOILETS

There are few public toilets and these are not normally kept to an acceptable standard. Use the hotel toilets. If there is a rubbish bin by the side of the toilet it is there to be used. Please do not put paper down the toilet unless there is no bin provided.

RESTAURANTS — AUTHORS' TOP TEN

The list that follows is a compilation of our favourite restaurants. These establishments serve good quality local food and are frequented on a regular basis by us!

Erol's
☎ 815 3657, Ozanköy village. Run by Erol Baha and his English wife Caroline. They serve the most delicious chicken kebab, sea bream and lamb chops all grilled over charcoal. The views from the roof terrace over the village of Ozanköy are breathtaking, especially on a balmy summers night watching the sun go down.

Ayna
☎ 815 1027, on the Bellapais approach road.
Excellent full kebab and a very well stocked bar. The *Katmer* (Turkish sweet pastry) must be sampled. The balcony has marvellous views over Girne.

Grapevine
☎ 815 2496, Girne. Local ducks, reared by the landlord Ketço (Jimmy) are a speciality of the house. This bar is a great favourite with the ex-pats and information for SpoT (Turtles) can be found here.

Anı
☎ 824 4355, Çatalköy. This is where the locals go for really good fish. The meze is all produced by the restaurant's own market garden. Speciality is *Tuzlu Balik* a large fish baked in rock salt. **MUST be pre-ordered**.

Ak Deniz
☎ 378 8227, travel north past Salamis ruins. A traditional taverna serving full kebab and if available try the molohiya and calamari.

Theresa
☎ 374 4368, 4 miles (7km) beyond Yenierenköy. A small friendly hotel and restaurant, situated on the north coast serving simple, fresh local fare.

Yeni Han
☎ 815 1276, western Girne, opposite Ship Inn. Serves an excellent choice of *Pide*, which is a bread base with various toppings and *Lah-macun*, known as Turkish Pizza.

Veranda
☎ 822 2053, Karaoğlanoğlu. A super beach setting with a varied menu. Good *Kleftico*.

Rose Gardens
☎ 815 3862, Ozanköy village. About 20 different hot and cold meze are served followed by a kebab of your choice. The meze is a meal in itself!

Set Fish
☎ 815 2336, Girne Harbour. In a wonderful position. The Hellim cheese is cooked to perfection, and the aubergine salad is delicious. Ask what the fresh fish of the day is.

SHOPPING

The two main shopping areas are Girne and Lefkoşa. There is an abundance of fake designer clothes from Levis to Armani to Calvin Klein. Look carefully as the quality varies greatly from shop to shop. Jewellery is a good buy. Each piece is weighed before a price is given. Basket ware is reasonable but the larger articles can be difficult to transport. It is an offence to take antiquities out of the country.

TELEPHONE SERVICES

All accommodations offer a facility for calling overseas. There is a 3 minute minimum charge followed by a rate per minute. This can be expensive. Check with reception for the tariff. A more economical way is to use the public boxes which are situated next to the Telecommunications Office in Girne, opposite the main post office. Simply insert your Visa/MasterCard credit card and dial the number. Code for UK is 0044. Remove the zero of the area code e.g. 0044 208 222 4444.

TIME

Northern Cyprus is two hours ahead of GMT in winter and three hours ahead of GMT in summer.

TIPPING

Although not expected, hotel staff, waiters and guides do appreciate a small gratuity. Some European-type restaurants will show a cover charge, if not, 10 per cent is normal.

TOURIST INFORMATION

If on a package tour, the representative of the tour company makes hotel visits. Take advantage of this most useful service as it can save you precious holiday time. The hotel staff can also be a great help with useful recommendations. The Tourist Information Centres are situated:

Girne
Hurriyet Caddesi, 200 yards (180m) past Dorana Hotel on the left.

Lefkoşa
On the main road from Girne into the city centre, at the second set of traffic lights on the left.

Gazimağusa
Fevzi Çakmak Bulvari, on the right-hand side towards the shipyard.

TRAVEL IN NORTHERN CYPRUS

Driving

Cyprus is a wonderful place to explore. Driving is easy, Cypriots drive on the left and the roads are blissfully uncongested. Red number plates distinguish hire cars. The main roads are usually in good condition, but may not be like the highways you are used to. Getting to where you want to go is often half the fun!

The amount of dual carriageways is slowly increasing to speed the flow of traffic between Lefkoşa, Girne and Gazimağusa. Minor roads are usually metalled, but can be narrow, winding and mountainous. For this reason it is a good idea not to equate mileage with driving time. *Wearing of front seatbelts is the law.* If you require rear seatbelts for your children check with the hire car company as they do not come as standard.

Speed restrictions are shown in kilometres, just take your time and enjoy the scenery. A rough guide is 50kmph (30mph) in a built up area and 95kmph (60mph) on the open road. Watch your speed. The police stand on the side of the roads with laser guns and will issue an on-the-spot fine. Cypriots sometimes flash their headlights to warn of a police check ahead.

Ask whether the car runs on leaded or unleaded fuel. Petrol stations are open from 8am-10.30pm, and once you are out of the main areas, can be few and far between, especially those selling unleaded petrol so make sure you start your journey with a full tank. Petrol is significantly cheaper than in the UK.

Look out for traffic lights that just constantly flash the red or amber light, this indicates that a filter system is in operation and you may proceed with caution.

The drink driving regulations are similar to England. A hefty on-the-spot fine is applicable.

As a general rule you can park where there is a space. Restricted areas are marked with either a no parking sign or black-and-white or yellow-and-white painted kerbstones. These are the same as double yellow lines. Car parks are called **Oto Parks**.

Drivers here tend not to use their indicators quite as consciously as on continental Europe, so be aware of the vehicle in front of you suddenly disappearing off to the left or the right. Horns are frequently used especially when overtaking.

It is necessary to file a police report if you have an accident. If you do not carry this out your car insurance will be null and void. Make sure you contact your rental company as well.

Most road signs are easily recognisable although worded in Turkish (see overleaf).

Dur	Stop
Dikkat	Attention
Girilmez	No entry
Yavaş	Slow
Yol Yapim	Roadworks
Askeri Bölge	Military Area
Yasak Bölge	Forbidden Zone
Fotograf Çekilmez	Photography Not Permitted

An amber flashing light on a high pole indicates that you are approaching a set of traffic lights, so slow down. At night some of the traffic lights are switched off, and just the middle amber light will be flashing. This means proceed with care. Painted oil drums are the sign that you are passing through or near an army base.

Public Transport

Each bus route is leased privately from the Government. The vehicles are all different shapes, sizes and colours with the end destination shown in the front windscreen. Locally called *Dolmuş*, which means stuffed, and you will understand why when you travel on one.

Either stand at a bus stop or simply flag the vehicle down anywhere along the road. This type of transport runs between the main towns and villages from approximately 6am-6pm. However there are no timetables so ask the driver the time of the return bus. Have some small change ready. Do not expect to get around the island on public transport. The buses do not go to many of the main attractions like Bellapais or St Hilarion Castle.

Taxis

A taxi is never far away, wherever you may be. All use an official tariff, which is Government controlled. The driver is obliged to show you the tariff when asked. Make sure you ask how much the journey will cost before departure. Most taxi drivers speak some English. The accommodations and restaurants normally have their own 'pet' taxi driver. Taxis are usually luxurious Mercedes saloons and display a yellow 'TAKSI' sign on the roof. There are also stretch types, which can carry up to 7 persons.

WALKING

Mid-summer is much too hot for this pastime, and the island is not at its best for people who enjoy flora and fauna. Even the mountain temperatures prove too high for most people. The best times are spring and early summer and then again in October and November. The ministry has marked out various trails, but these can prove difficult to follow.

Recently a book has been published called *Walks in Northern Cyprus*. It is well laid out and contains 15 different walks, which will appeal to strong and 'weekend' walkers alike. Available from Green Jacket Bookshop, Girne.

WATER

The water in Northern Cyprus is usually potable, but bottled water can be purchased from the restaurants, shops and accommodations.

WATER SPORTS

There is a variety of watersports on offer at **Deniz Kızı beach** and **LA beach**. Some diving schools operate out of the old harbour, offering professional advance diving instruction courses. Please read your holiday insurance before undertaking any sporting activity.

WEATHER AND WHEN TO GO

As the most easterly of the Mediterranean islands, Cyprus is consequently the driest and hottest. The temperature starts to build up in May and by July and August it is in the 30s to 40s°C (80-100°F) on the coast. Inland it is normally three to five degrees higher.

It is necessary to be well-protected from the sun's ultraviolet rays. Have plenty of sun screen, sunglasses and a hat. There is very little chance of rain from May to October unless there is an atmospheric build up and a spectacular thunderstorm breaks and clears the air.

Swimmers will be pleased to know that the sea is warm from early June to the end of October. Winter bathing is only for the hardy, most people prefer indoor heated swimming pools.

An important consideration is the cut-off point between reliable weather and the possibility of bad. If swimming and sunbathing is what you want from your holiday, with evenings spent dining outside, then November through to April is out. Most of the restaurants do not move their seating outside until May.

There is certain to be rain from December through to March and it is dark early, making the days short. Winter evenings are cold and it is important to remember that few establishments (apart from hotels) have modern heating systems. Most Cypriots light the open fire and put an extra jumper on! This is not to say that the winter months should be avoided. The days are normally clear and sunny with fantastic views across to the Turkish mountains, which are lost in the heat haze of summer.

April is the month to witness the famous Cyprus spring when the landscape is transformed into a blaze of colour. It can rain at this time of the year, but it can also be wonderfully warm. This is a good time to tour and see the historical sites before the heat sets in, or October when things are starting to cool down again. From June the green plains turn to a dusty brown.

LANDMARK VISITORS

(See page 175 for mailing details)

Cornwall
& the Isles of Scilly

Rita Tregellas Pope

Cornwall
ISBN: 1 901522 09 1
256pp, full colour
£10.95

Devon

Brian Le Messurier

Devon
ISBN: 1 901522 42 3
224pp, full colour
£9.95

Guernsey
Alderney, Sark & Herm

David Greenwood

Guernsey
ISBN: 1 901522 48 2
224pp, full colour
£9.95

Jersey

Sonia Hillsdon

Jersey
ISBN: 1 901522 47 4
224pp, full colour
£9.99

Dorset

Richard Sale

Dorset
ISBN: 1 901522 46 6
240pp, full colour
£9.95

Somerset

Richard Sale

Somerset
ISBN: 1 901522 40 7
224pp, full colour
£10.95

Hampshire
& The Isle of Wight

John Barton

Hampshire
ISBN: 1 901522 14 8
224pp, full colour
£9.95

Cotswolds
& Shakespeare Country

Richard Sale

Cotswolds
ISBN: 1 901522 12 1
224pp, full colour
£9.99

Peak District

Lindsey Porter

Peak District
ISBN: 1 901522 25 3
240pp, full colour
£9.99

East Anglia

Norman & June Buckley

East Anglia
ISBN: 1 901522 58 X
224pp, full colour
£9.95

Yorkshire Dales

Ron Scholes

Yorkshire Dales
ISBN: 1 901522 41 5
224pp, full colour
£10.95

GUIDES TO THE UK

Lake District
ISBN: 1 901522 38 5
224pp, full colour
£9.95

Scotland
ISBN: 1 901522 18 0
288pp, full colour
£11.95

Harrogate
ISBN: 1 901522 55 5
96pp, full colour
£4.95

West Cornwall
ISBN: 1 901522 24 5
96pp, full colour
£5.95

South Devon
ISBN: 1 901522 52 0
96pp, full colour
£5.95

Southern Peak
ISBN: 1 901522 27 X
96pp, full colour
£5.95

Southern Lakeland
ISBN: 1 901522 53 9
96pp, full colour
£5.95

Dartmoor
ISBN: 1 901522 69 5
96pp, full colour
£5.95

New Forest
ISBN: 1 901522 70 9
96pp, full colour
£5.95

Isle of Wight
ISBN: 1 901522 71 7
256pp, full colour
£5.95

Hereford
ISBN: 1 901522 72 5
96pp, full colour
£5.95

Prices subject to alteration from time to time

Acropolis – Ancient city fortification usually on a hilltop

Agora – Public square, market and meeting place of a town or city

Ambulatory – The aisle that runs behind the altar at the eastern end of the church

Apse – Semi-circular or polygonal termination at the east end of the church

Arcade – Row of arches resting on columns

Ashlar – Masonry of finely dressed stone

Atrium – Forecourt or entrance to a villa or basilica

Barbican – Defences in front of a main entrance

Basilica – A large hall used for judicial and commercial purposes; a magnificent church formed out of such a hall

Belvedere – An open, often roofed structure, usually elevated, providing a good viewpoint

Capital – Capstone, ornamental carved of a column

Corbel – Block projecting from a wall to support weight

Dorter – Sleeping quarters in a monastery ie. dormitory

Dromos – Ramp leading to underground entrance of a tomb

Enceinte – The walls surrounding a castle

Gargoyle – Ornamental water spout

Hypocaust – Underground space through which hot air is circulated to provide heating for baths, sweating rooms and central heating for villas.

Iconastasis – The altar screen in an orthodox church

Machicolations – External gallery or parapet with holes in the floor through which missiles could be dropped on an enemy below

Minaret – The tower attached to a mosque from which the muezzin makes his call to prayer

Nave – The main central aisle of a church

Opus sectile – Ornamental pattern of squared or polygonally cut stones usually marble or granite and laid as flooring

Orchestra – The semi-circular area of a theatre in which the Greeks performed their dramas

Panayia – The Blessed Virgin Mary

Peristyle – Columned walkway surrounding a courtyard

Plinth – Pedestal base of a column

Refectory – Dining hall, usually in an ecclesiastical building, eg. abbey or monastery

Roof boss – Carved ornament at the junction of the roof vaulting ribs

Synthronon – The semi-circle of seats for the clergy in the main apse of a Byzantine orthodox church

Temenos – Sacred area within a boundary, specifically a sanctuary of pagan times

Tesserae – Usually small cubes of naturally coloured rock, or hand-coloured and kiln-fired ceramic, that are used to make up the patterns of a mosaic

Tracery – Ornamental carvings much used in Gothic architecture, dividing the sections of windows and arches

Transept – The transverse section, joining nave and sanctuary, to be found in most churches

Tympanum – The semi-circular flat surface above a door or window lintel and below the arch, often painted with small icons, scenes of martyrdom etc.

Undercroft – Usually a vaulted room for stores below ground level in a monastery or abbey. Bellapais abbey has a fine example.

LANDMARK
VISITORS GUIDES

US & British VI
ISBN: 1 901522 03 2
256pp, full colour
£11.95

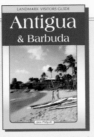

Antigua & Barbuda
ISBN: 1 901522 02 4
96pp, full colour
£5.95

Bermuda
ISBN: 1 901522 07 5
160pp, full colour
£7.95

Dominican Republic
ISBN: 1 90152208 3
160pp, full colour
£7.95

Pack 2 months
into 2 weeks
with your

Landmark
Visitors Guides

New Zealand
ISBN:
1 901522 36 9
320pp, full colour
£12.95

Iceland
ISBN: 1 901522 68 7
192pp, full colour
£10.95

Orlando
ISBN:
1 901522 22 9
256pp, full colour
£9.95

Florida: Gulf Coast
ISBN:
1 901522 01 6
160pp, full colour
£7.95

Florida: The Keys
ISBN:
1 901522 21 0
160pp, full colour
£7.95

St Lucia
ISBN:
1 901522 28 8
144pp, full colour
£6.95

Provence
ISBN: 1 901522 45 8
240pp, full colour
£10.95

Côte d'Azur
ISBN: 1 901522 29 6
112pp, full colour
£6.50

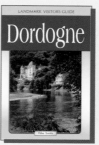

Dordogne
ISBN: 1 901522 67 9
224pp, full colour
£11.95

Madeira
ISBN: 1 901522 42 3
192pp, full colour
£8.95

Italian Lakes
ISBN: 1 901522 11 3
240pp, full colour
£11.95

Bruges
ISBN: 1 901522 66 0
112pp, full colour
£5.95

Riga
ISBN: 1 901522 59 8
160pp, full colour
£8.95

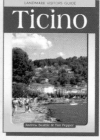

Ticino
ISBN: 1 901522 74 1
192pp, full colour
£8.95

Cracow
ISBN: 1 901522 54 7
160pp, full colour
£7.95

India: Goa
ISBN: 1 901522 23 7
160pp, full colour
£7.95

India: Kerala
ISBN: 1 901522 16 4
256pp, full colour
£10.99

Sri Lanka
ISBN: 1 901522 37 7
192pp, full colour
£9.95

Prices subject to alteration from time to time

THE AUTHORS

Both authors live in Northern Cyprus and both are involved in the travel industry. Kristina Gürsoy graduated in hotel management and moved to Northern Cyprus where she met and married her Turkish Cypriot husband. Together they have built Kıbrıs Travel Services into one of the leading car hire and tourist handling agencies. Lavinia Neville Smith escaped from the UK rat race after a varied career in such diverse occupations as market research, Land and Range Rover sales and the field of aviation.

Published by
Landmark Publishing Ltd,
Waterloo House, 12 Compton, Ashbourne, Derbyshire DE6 1DA England
Tel: (01335) 347349 Fax: (01335) 347303 e-mail: landmark@clara.net

ISBN 1 901 522 51 2

Print: Gutenberg Press Ltd, Malta
Editor: Pamela Hopkinson
Cartography & design: Samantha Witham

Front cover: Lala Mustapha Paşa Mosque (St Nicholas), Gazimağusa
Back cover, top: Ayios Philon, Dipkarpaz
Back cover, bottom: Kyrenia harbour

Picture Credits
All photographs have been kindly supplied by
Eberhard Seliger except the following:
The authors: Back cover bottom, 27, 51 both, 66, 107B, 134T, 142T
Mr Axel Neuhaus: 22T